MYSTICAL
INTERLUDES II

A Collection of Ordinary People's Mystical Experiences

MYSTICAL INTERLUDES II

A Collection of Ordinary People's Mystical Experiences

Collected and Edited by

Emily Rodavich

Interior design: Penelope Love · *Cover design:* Rolf Busch

Library of Congress Cataloging-in-Publication Data

Rodavich, Emily
Mystical Interludes II: A Collection of Ordinary People's
Mystical Experiences

p. cm.
Paperback ISBN: 978-1-947708-18-1
Ebook ISBN: 978-1-947708-19-8
Library of Congress Control Number: 2018952697

10 9 8 7 6 5 4 3 2 1
First Edition, October 2018

CITRINE PUBLISHING
Asheville, North Carolina, U.S.A.
(828) 585-7030
Publisher@CitrinePublishing.com
www.CitrinePublishing.com

*To all who question the meaning of life and
are fearless enough to search for truth*

"*A lost coin is found by means of a candle; the deepest truth is found by means of a simple story.*"

—Anthony de Mello

TABLE OF CONTENTS

TABLE OF CONTENTS

TABLE OF CONTENTS

TABLE OF CONTENTS

FOREWORD

Suzanne Giesemann

Who doesn't love magical stories? Most of us as children delighted in hearing fanciful fairytales filled with magic. As we grew older and our lives became filled with work, family, and other responsibilities, the fairy tales became something we tucked away in our memories. Occasionally, however, we still experience moments of wonder and connection that defy explanation. The uniqueness and rarity of these moments give us the feeling that we're witness to some kind of miracle.

But what exactly is a miracle? Technically, it is an extraordinary event in the physical world that surpasses all known human or natural powers.[1] I used to view miracles that way, until I discovered that this physical world is but one reality in the multidimensional universe of which we are a part. After a full career as a naval officer, during which I experienced no greater or fewer miracles than most of my other colleagues, I discovered through meditation the existence of the greater reality.

I discovered that our loved ones who have passed still exist at a level beyond our own. As the title of my latest book declares, those who have shed their earthly bodies are *Still Right Here*, and they continue to exert an influence in our lives. I learned that beyond the spirit world, there are worlds within worlds inhabited by even greater aspects of the Infinite Intelligence that guides all life.

---

1 http://www.dictionary.com/browse/miracle

With this awareness, and with my now daily interaction with the greater reality, I have a new understanding of miracles. A miracle is when the world beyond this physical world intersects with our own in a way we can't ignore. Magical moments don't lose their wonder, but they are no longer "magical" in the sense of being some kind of deceptive illusion. The illusion is that this world is the only reality.

Emily Rodavich has experienced numerous miracles in her life, and she shared them beautifully in her first book, *Mystical Interludes*. Emily gifted me with her book when we met at a class I was teaching on how to connect with those across the veil. A relentless nudge caused me to set aside another book I had taken for my bedtime reading. That evening, I began reading Emily's memoir. In spite of knowing I had to get up early for the second day of class, I had to force myself to put her book down well after midnight.

What was it that kept me turning the pages of that first book? It was the perfect combination of Emily's dramatic life story, the beautiful light of her soul that shined through each word, and the magical stories—what she calls "mystical interludes"—that led her to shine so brightly. I recognized in Emily a kindred spirit—a woman who has lifted the veil and knows that it is love that connects all of us with All That Is.

How pleased I was to learn that Emily had compiled a collection of others' mystical interludes. I know from my own research that simply by reading other people's other-worldly experiences, we are more likely to experience such events ourselves. How exciting! Thanks to the gift of *Mystical Interludes II*, now you and others who read this new volume of stories may be able to contribute your own stories to a future volume!

And why not? As you will discover in these pages, mystical interludes are not reserved for those with particular beliefs or attitudes. Those who have so generously shared their stories in this delightful collection are "real" people ... the guy and girl next door with whom we can easily identify. Their stories will draw you in with their humanity. Just as I found it hard to put down Emily's first book, the stories Emily has compiled for this second volume will make it hard for you to stop reading.

Why this urge for "just one more" story? Because mystical interludes give us hope. They affirm our inner awareness that we are part of something far greater than our earthly lives with their many challenges. Savor every "magical" moment you will read in this treasure of a book. See in these sacred stories the influence of a loving Universe trying to bring our attention to the fact that this life is not all there is. Hold in your awareness the fact that magic is all around you when you have the eyes to see and ears to hear.

I'm grateful to Emily and to those whose stories you are about to enjoy for helping to open our eyes to the beautiful web of life of which we are a part.

Blessings!

Suzanne Giesemann
June 2018

INTRODUCTION

Emily Rodavich

Have you ever had a mystical interlude?
"What is that?" many people ask with furrowed brow.

This is an everyday conversation for me now, but it wasn't always. Several years ago, I sat down to write for my grand-children stories of the inexplicable events of my life, and each mystical event sprang to life in all my senses as though I were living it for the first time. Having kept those stories to myself for fear of ridicule, I was astonished to realize their virtues and the multifold ways they have shaped my life.

In short, my mystical interludes have enabled me to live my daily life fearlessly with joyful gratitude. They inured in me a deep faith in our Creator, taught me forgiveness, demonstrated that Love is eternal, eradicated my fear of death, and expanded my consciousness. I have often commented that I am one of the happiest people I know.

But don't think of me as a Pollyanna. I was born into poverty, endured abuse as a child, and suffered from painful, ugly allergies, which caused my hands, feet and face to break out. Later in life I experienced a heart-breaking divorce, which left me penniless to fend for myself and my three children, and I have had to work hard most of my life.

Becoming aware of the amazing benefits of my mystical experiences, I began talking about them and soon discovered that just about everybody I talked with had experienced magical events, some similar to mine. Like me, they rarely talked about them. This inspired me to compile some of my stories into a memoir. From that moment, I felt the wind at my back as the manuscript took flight.

When the writing was complete, a good friend *conveniently* introduced me to an outstanding editor, Penelope Love, who later became my accomplished publisher. My next challenge was titling the book. After filling many tablet pages with unimpressive brainstorming attempts, two words *dropped* into my mind as I stood in a warm shower one morning: *Mystical Interludes.* The word mystical means something that inspires awe, and interlude means an intervening period of time or space. My first book, *Mystical Interludes: An Ordinary Person's Extraordinary Experiences* was born.

At the end of the book I share the many benefits from my extraordinary events. I have come to believe that everybody has mystical experiences, and realizing the importance of talking and writing about them, I invite readers to submit stories of their experiences for publication in this book. Recalling how challenging it was for me at age eighteen to explain to my mother that I had died and visited heaven, I also encourage readers to use the term *mystical interlude* to refer to most types of unexplainable happenings. I'll never forget how excited and relieved I was, almost twenty years after my near death, when Dr. Raymond Moody coined the term *near-death experience!* Until then, I secretly wondered if I were the only living person to experience such a thing. It's my deepest hope that the term *mystical interlude* will facilitate and normalize sharing stories, not only in private, but in social circles as well.

Mystical interludes can range from minor incidents, to which we may never give a second thought, to mind-boggling, unexplainable happenings. A most common type of mystical interlude is *coincidence.* We use this word habitually, but how often do we consider its meaning? Think about it. A coincidence is an occurrence which spontaneously manifests in our personal time and space, leaving us in wonderment.

Some coincidences are merely pleasant happenstances, whereas others have significant meanings or destinies woven into them. A trivial example of the latter might be that of a person in a great hurry for an important event. Approaching a parking meter, he suddenly realizes he has no change or means for paying the fee. At that moment he sees a coin on the sidewalk, the exact coin needed. This coincidence has definite meaning for him. Whether or not he attributes it to divine intervention, it most certainly brings him a sigh of relief, if not a small moment of gratitude.

A more dramatic example, further along the spectrum of universal significance, happened to an acquaintance of mine. He had a seizure while driving. His speeding vehicle crashed into a concrete obstacle, rolled over and caught fire. The unconscious driver was pinned under his dashboard while strapped into his seat. Coincidentally, the driver of the car behind him was a man who had been trained as a first responder. Not only did this person know rescue procedures, he also carried equipment for breaking car windows and slashing seatbelts. This *coincidence* saved the driver. *What made it happen? Does it have meaning?* There's little doubt that the victim thinks so.

Mystical interludes cut across religion, politics, ethnicity, and nationality. They occur in myriad ways such as *synchronicities, gut feelings, significant dreams, intuitions, signs, precognitions, visions, and out-of-body and near-death experiences.* What makes them mystical is that these experiences are not understood by the mind. Thinking about them often makes us uncomfortable because they stymie reasoning and rational understanding. Rather, they resonate in our hearts, sometimes in our souls, leaving us with a *knowing* that something *real* has happened.

On Honoring and Sharing Our Mystical Interludes

MY MISSION IS TO ENCOURAGE people everywhere to become aware and mindful of mystical interludes when they occur. I believe they are Divinity's way of reminding us of who we *really* are: spiritual beings in human bodies.

If you doubt the truth of the last statement, consider the needs of a newborn. It "cannot live on bread alone." If a newborn human were nothing more than a new physical body, it would thrive on bodily sustenance alone. But that's not the case. Its spirit must also be nourished—with love. What can be more spiritual than giving and receiving love? The Bible says "God is Love." Babies deprived of love wither, and most die. The ones who survive are typically debilitated by cognitive, behavioral or psychological dysfunctions. To verify these facts, you might wish to search the Internet for "babies deprived of love."

As we grow from infancy, and our egos and individuality develop, we begin to perceive ourselves as physical persons separate from *other* human beings. Our need for love is met through relationships with family, friends, romantic partners, nature and perhaps also from our Source of Being/God/Spirit/ Universe or another chosen name for It. We can become mentally and emotionally consumed as we strive to attain personal goals and success, focusing on the body, personal appearance, possessions, status, and daily schedules. Meanwhile, the expression of who we really are—spiritual beings—can become stifled. A mystical interlude, which resonates in the heart, can remind us of our spirituality and our connectedness to each other. This is why it is meaningful to take heed.

An important insight from my experience is this: the more I acknowledge and share my mystical interludes with others, the more they occur to enhance my life. A perfect example is my *coincidental* meeting with outstanding medium and author, Suzanne Giesemann.

My friend Nancy and I attended Suzanne's invaluable *Serving Spirit* workshop in October 2017. We had a room at the resort where the class was located and planned to leave on Sunday afternoon after it ended. At the last minute, Nancy and I decided to stay another night.

As we entered the dining room the following morning, we were quite surprised to see Suzanne sitting alone at a table! We assumed she had departed for home the previous day after ending her session. Seeing us, she smiled broadly and invited us to her table saying, "I knew you would be here this morning. I was waiting for you."

We were stunned and delighted! I was even more surprised when she said to me, "I read half your book last night and had a hard time putting it down."

During the weekend, I had gifted her a book thinking she might never get around to reading it with her demanding schedule. As a result of that mystical interlude Suzanne has honored me by writing the foreword to this, my second book.

One of the best ways to fully realize a mystical interlude is to share it openly with others, preferably soon afterwards. Talking about it revives it within you and also authenticates it. As you become comfortable talking about your spontaneous mystical events and hearing those of others you will find your world expanding. Your heart will likely expand as well.

I have found evidence of this from personal experience. Giving book talks at libraries I discovered that people wanted to stay afterwards and talk about their own mystical interludes. These lingering crowds inspired me to start the Mystical Interludes Discussion Group (MIDG), which invites open-minded individuals of all socio-religious backgrounds to meet each month and share their experiences. Those who attend regularly become increasingly tuned to noticing mystical interludes as they occur in their lives. Sharing those experiences is normalized within the group. A common bond, which transcends religion, politics, race and other segregators, grows within the group, cultivating fertile ground for friendship and love.

I ask myself what would happen beyond our smaller circles if everyone were to openly share their mystical interludes with others? In doing so perhaps we could expand our spiritual selves and abate divisions that separate our human family into polarized groups. If we are ever to have world peace, it will not come through war, government, politics or religion. Publishing the mystical interludes of other ordinary people like myself is my effort to aid and support that spiritual awareness.

The stories in this book are written and shared openly by people from various backgrounds. You will hear the voice of each person in the telling. Occasionally a writer's religious views might be reflected; however, the sharing of these stories involves no religious agenda whatsoever. Mystical interludes happen—and have happened from the beginning of time—in the contexts of all faiths and belief systems.

Authors and their stories are arranged in no particular order, similar to the unpredictable encounters and experiences that pattern the course of our lives. An astounding account might be followed by one that evokes a heart-felt resonance, or even a smile. Each person's voice will shine through his or her narrative.

Attempting to compare one person's experience with another's would be as meaningless as comparing lines in their fingerprints. Just as each of us is an original one-of-a-kind being, each story is a unique, authentic revelation. The common thread throughout these narratives is that they are *real*. That reality is evidenced by their influences on their writers' lives.

My purpose and hope is that as you read these accounts, you will be inspired to examine your own life more closely for similar spontaneous events, then talk about them with friends and acquaintances. You might even consider submitting them for publication in Mystical Interludes III. The more aware we become of the *reality* of our own spiritual selves and those of others, the more we can nullify manmade divisions among our human family, divisions which can be adversarial or hostile, and allow a powerful bond to fill in the spaces between us.

To borrow from a popular aphorism, I am committed to the belief that a rising spiritual tide can lift all hearts to Love. A powerful tool for churning that tide is the mystical interlude. May these true stories instill in you new insights into humanity's spiritual reality and open your heart to all-embracing love, trust, connection, healing and joy.

Interlude with Eternity

Bonnie Bassan

Indian Paintbrush,
vermillion lined with yellow
Mexican Hat,
jaunty and jocular
A triple rainbow
majestic and elusive,
the hum and twitter
of the red chin hummingbird
A boulder cracks loudly
cleanly in two
crashes through the wilderness
rolls twenty feet
ripping the pine branch from its trunk
it splits into two again
Centered by the tactile
touching, smelling
drinking in beauty through the
chalice of my eyes
sipping through the pores of my skin
the world that I am a small but significant part of
a puddle of appreciation
transpires into
a monsoon of gratitude
blows through my entire body
emerges through my tears

joys of tears,
libation on the soil
gentleness hovers in the
spaces between the breath
The grandeur and awe
nature is poetry
I am the artifice and the artisan
I touch my father through the wet dirt,
feel his heart beating in the red clay in my hands
When mushrooms broke free from the earth,
he nourished me
My mother too lives in the fleeting orange day lily
beauty here but a day
Ballast, these moments of Beauty
seep into Joy,
cannot be contained,
in the vessel of my soul
In these increments of time
I arrive at eternity,
and break free of the prison of time, death and grief

Bonnie Bassan is a yoga instructor/bankruptcy lawyer who recently reconnected with her love for poetry and writing. Rediscovering poetry was like finding a long lost piece of herself. She lives in New Mexico and teaches yoga to at risk youth in the public schools. She plans to bring yoga and writing to the schools on a larger scale to help youths connect with emotional literacy. She is currently finishing a memoir about her own troubled childhood and finding love and joy through yoga.

The Right Choice

Ann Miller

My name is Ann. I live a rather ordinary life in a small town in Pennsylvania and have raised four children. Now I am blessed with lots of grandchildren…even several great-grandchildren.

Many years have passed since I experienced this mystical interlude. The memory is still very vivid for me. I like sharing my story because it has had a major impact on my life. Maybe it will help others to reflect on an incident they have had that changed—or could have changed their lives.

Back in the '50s when I was a sophomore at a University in Lewisburg, Pennsylvania, I was in love with Tom, a senior. Living nearby, I commuted to school from home each day. Tom shared an apartment on campus with his fraternity brothers, Gary and Stan. Tom and I had been a couple for quite some time. I wore his fraternity pin as a way of indicating that we were in a serious, dedicated relationship.

On this particular evening, my mother was preparing a special dinner for my brother, Chet, who had been home on a short leave from his naval base in Philadelphia. Chet was due to report back at base the following morning. We wanted Tom to join us for Chet's last night of leave.

Following my afternoon class that day, I jumped into my car and stopped by Tom's apartment to invite him to come home with me. I was disappointed to find nobody there. A little dejected, I left and headed out of town.

Approaching the stop sign at a main intersection, I signaled left toward home and suddenly heard a voice commanding me to go back! It came out of nowhere. Nobody was around. I paused and listened.

The voice distinctly commanded, "Go back!"

I sat for a moment, puzzled and confused. Then I was compelled to turn right and drive back to the apartment.

To my surprise, Tom answered the door. When I invited him to come home with me for dinner with my family, he frowned disappointedly because he had volunteered to pass out programs at the basketball game that night. Also, one of his roommates, Stan, would not be home for dinner, and Tom didn't want to abandon his other roommate, Gary, to eating dinner alone.

Just as I was about to leave, disappointed for the second time, Tom's friend Bill stopped by. Bill heard us lamenting about Tom's having to miss dinner at my house, so he came to the rescue. He said he'd eat at the apartment with Gary and afterwards go with Gary to the basketball game.

"Stan might get back in time to go with us," Bill added. "We can pile into Gary's convertible."

We decided that I'd return Tom to campus later so he could distribute programs at the game, and I would study at the library. With that settled, Tom and I left for dinner with my family.

Much later that night when I returned home from the library, the telephone was ringing as I entered the house. I knew my parents had taken my brother to meet his ride for the Naval base, so I ran to answer before the caller hung up.

One of Tom's fraternity brothers was on the line. "Is Tom with you?" he asked.

"No." I answered. "Why?"

"When did you last see him?"

"Why? What's up?" I asked.

"There's been a terrible accident on the way to the game... Gary's car was hit by a fast-moving train."

"What?" I was stunned by this shocking news, "Where ..."

"It happened at an unmarked crossing in town," he said, "Gary and Bill were both killed. Stan was thrown clear. He's still alive with bad injuries."

"Oh no!" I gasped.

"The guys here at the frat house know that Tom usually goes to the games with Gary and Stan. We're worried that he might have been in Gary's car. Do you know where he is?"

I told him of our evening together at my house, and that I had left Tom at the gym to pass out programs. I was sure he had not been with his roommates and Bill at that time. Shocked and concerned myself, I knew Tom would be devastated when he got the news.

These many years later, I remain saddened by the tragic deaths of Gary and Bill. At the same time, I'm thankful that I heeded that mysterious voice.

"Go back!" it commanded. Had I had not listened and acted on what I heard, Tom would most likely be dead.

Tom has been my husband for sixty-one years.

I am most grateful for my life-saving mystical interlude!

Editor's Note: This story came through MysticalInterludes.com. Ann Miller and I have never met, but from her writing and through our email communications, I know her as an intelligent, grateful, and compassionate person. Ann clearly cares enough to share her experience with hope that it might benefit others.

A Special Delivery

Jan Lawrence

This story starts before I was born. My mother Jeanette had two very difficult pregnancies with my older brothers, Brad and John. Later, she had a miscarriage. Her doctors cautioned her about getting pregnant again, but her desire to have a daughter overtook their advice. During her pregnancy with me, Mom lived with my paternal grandmother, Lessie, whose claim to fame was that she was the second successful brain-hemorrhage surgery in the United States, the first being actress Patricia Neal. Looking back, I believe God had plans for her.

Granny Lessie cared for my pregnant mother, who was confined to bed rest for most of nine months because of persistent toxemia. I was born at last via C-section in Cleveland, Ohio, on July 30, 1964. Tragically, my mother died eight days later from a surgical complication during my birth.

My brothers and I were left without a mother. My father, now a widower, had no idea how to raise three children on his own. We lived with Granny for the first several years of my life. She became the pivotal person in my existence. By the time I reached age seven, my family consisted of my dad, a stepmother, two brothers and three step-brothers. We left Ohio and moved to Avella, Pennsylvania, a rural coal-mining town.

I survived the school years by returning to Cleveland every summer to be with my beloved grandmother, who taught me about God, music, and love. She was God's blessing to me in our loss. When I was in my twenties, my aging granny moved close to her daughter in Florida. I was devastated.

Fast forward to January 2000. I was in my ninth month of pregnancy when I learned that Granny was moving from Florida back to our original home of Ohio. I was ecstatic with excitement, not only for the birth of my baby, but also because Granny would be living nearby again!

But death darkened my life once more. The day before she was to move, my beloved granny died unexpectedly of a heart attack! That was on January 25, 2000.

On January 29, I went into labor, terrified and grieving. Having recently lost my grandmother and also having lost my mother during my own birth time, I was afraid of the birth process. At the same time, I knew it was inevitable. At hour twenty-six, with no progression of labor, I was given Pitocin. Rather than increase contractions, it worked opposite, causing the contractions to stop. I fell into a deep, deep sleep.

While there, this is what I remember. I entered a bright white room where my mother and grandmother were seated in chairs on one side of a long table. I don't recall what they were wearing, but their faces were as clear as if they were alive and well in human flesh right there in front of me. And I can't forget that brilliant white room! Granny had her familiar southern drawl as she told me they were right there with me. I never had the gift of hearing my mother's voice (except perhaps from the womb), but it was calm and soft just as I had imagined it. They were ageless. Mom was just 26 when she died, and she was as beautiful as my picture of her.

I sat in an empty chair across from them. My mother spoke, telling me it was time for me to get the baby out. I cried, telling them I could not do it without them. I might die just like Mom did. I didn't know how to be a parent.

Granny said, "We're right here with you."

Mom commanded, "Get up and get the baby out!"

My anxiety dissolved into determination.

The next thing I remember is being out of my hospital bed and pacing the room. My husband, asleep in the chair next to my bed, startled awake when he heard me jump out of bed. I walked back and forth frantically, repeating that Mom and Granny told me to "get up and get the baby out!"

My frenetic walking brought the needed contractions back. Within a few hours, I was holding my precious son, Robert.

I remember this experience vividly in its detail, grateful that it moved me to take immediate action. This encounter shattered my life-long fear that giving birth would lead to my death. I never wanted my child to grow up without a mother because it was so very difficult for my brothers and me.

My experience with Mom and Granny also instilled the courage in me to try pregnancy again. Now I also have a daughter who is as beautiful, loving and kind as my mom was.

I made a promise to God, Mom and Granny, that if I were able to stay with my kids for a while, I would teach them about God, music, and mostly about love. I work towards that every day that God's grace keeps my heart beating and my blood flowing. I only wish I could see or talk to Mom and Granny again; for I miss them every single day.

I'd love to hear them say, "I told you so."

Jan Lawrence is the loving wife of twenty-one years to Bob, mother of Robert, about to graduate from high school, and Erin, age thirteen. They live in the south hills of Pittsburgh with their little Malt-Zhu, Cookie. Jan works as both a church secretary and a library assistant. In her spare time, she sings, entertaining in senior facilities, skilled nursing centers, and occasional private functions. Jan believes that there is no such thing as coincidence. She takes time every day to thank God for her blessings.

Death is Not the Final Chorus

Chloe Rachel Gallaway

My life has been like no other, and yet, I remain connected to all of you in every way. I spent the first twelve years of my life in the wilderness.

It did not happen by chance, but rather by choice—although not my choice. I was born there. My father was a creative genius with big ideas and ideals of how we should live out our human existence. He was a man of the world, a known musician and songwriter who played alongside Janis Joplin and the greats, then left it all behind to create his own path, to leave his mark upon his children and upon the sacred land where he devoted his days to living.

As a child, I knew very little of the world, this strange place far removed from my everyday play among the red hills of clay. I knew only that I wasn't an Indian and I wasn't living in the seventeen or eighteen hundreds, but I was living just as those in the past had lived. Society was far in the distance: cars, buses, school, cities—they were not a part of my vocabulary, nor a part of my vision. And so you see, my connection was to the earth, to the trees, to the birds taking flight, to the wind blowing through my body—the song of nature sang to me daily. When you are born in the woods along with your five siblings, you and your siblings sing this song, a little different sound heard through each voice, but it's the shared song that becomes a rhythm of life. I lived in this rhythm with my siblings.

Nature is a devout teacher in her beauty, her twists and turns, her loss, her love and her ever-changing rhythm. One cannot be in bliss at all times walking the green path in the forest. I can't tell you all the stories here—there are so many, I've written a book about them, *The Soulful Child: Twelve Years in The Wilderness.* However, there is one story not told there in vivid detail. It is one that has molded my life, broken me open, and awakened me to matters of life and death. It is this story I'd like to share with you here.

I call my five siblings and me "The Pack." Like a pack of wolves, we ate together, worked, together, played together, and rode the winds of change together: John, Carey, Nye, Rose, Jacinth, and me—four boys and two girls. We had names but rarely used them, our energy bodies and non-verbal cues tagging us through the day. John was the eldest, strong and fierce, but kind and gentle. A protector of my mother, he had a deep soul with blue eyes lighting his strong cheek bones, and dark brown hair outlining his forehead. The world would call him "handsome."

He was opposite my father in many ways and the two of them had fought many battles by the time John turned fifteen. The rest of us listened to the loud voices rising up through the walls of the small cabin when they disagreed. It was August of 1983 and my father had gotten angry at John for carving his name in an Aspen tree that stood in a grove where they went to pick wild oregano and raspberries, a few miles up the mountain from our home. That day in the sacred woods of my childhood, John had taken to using his pocket knife to carve his name and a date in the tree. On the day of the carving it was August 1983, yet John had inscribed:

John Gallaway, October 1984

My father was livid that John had carved his name in the tree, but even more upset that he'd carved the wrong month and date. Why would he do that? Despite the fact that John had not attended traditional school, he was highly educated, reading four grade levels ahead of his age, and wise beyond his years. It made no sense.

The dance of father and son went on for a whole year. Together they trained wild horses that my father had rescued. Together they tried to work side by side, but their differences caught up to them and more arguments ensued. And then one day—silence—a break in the morning rays that streamed across the front yard. The particles of light split into golden streams bouncing off the ground, and John was gone. He had left before the sun came up.

A whole year had passed since John carved his name and the wrong date in the Aspen tree. It was September of 1984. We went about daily life that fall, the yellow oak leaves falling to the ground, the juniper and cedar trees smelling fragrant. My mother said John would come back. Days passed, and then weeks.

"When will he come back?" I asked my mother, while she read to us by kerosene lamp at night.

"He will come back," she assured me.

Another month passed, no John. That fall, winter arrived like she never had before; by October the ground was white with snow. We went to bed just after dark with the fire blazing in front of us for warmth; by midnight there were only coals keeping a faint heat in the room, which had thin boarded walls with no plaster. Around midnight I awoke to a strange sound and sat up in bed listening. Someone was driving up the mountain. We rarely had visitors and we never had visitors at night. My body was startled by the knowing of this.

I woke my father by calling out to him. "Dad... Dad... someone is coming." Both my mother and father got out of bed. We all waited in silence for the truck that bellowed up the steep hills onto our property. Finally the engine cut off in the front yard. My father exited the house, leaving the rest of us standing there. He came back within ten minutes. I watched him grab his black cowboy hat from the hat rack and lace his boots that had been left untied.

My older brother Carey raced to my father's side. "What's going on?" he pried.

My father's face was solemn as he looked down at his boots, "John is in the hospital," he answered.

We clambered around him with questions, Carey and my mother asking them out loud and the rest of us asking them in silence.

"I don't know what happened, I don't know the details," my father responded. "He was in an accident."

For my father, a man who had denounced the entire medical system, treating his children's illness homeopathically using herbs from the land, it was his worst nightmare. His son was now lying in a hospital bed somewhere in the city, the city he had long left with a hope of protecting his children from the sufferings of the world.

It was October 1984, the month and year John had carved in the tree. In the midst of trauma, we could not realize what it all meant. I can tell you that years later in the writing of my book, I finally came to realize what it all meant. I can tell you I will never forget that October, the coldest fall that ever blew in, and what it felt like to lose my brother. Our pack would never be the same; one of us wouldn't make it. One of us would be buried behind our cabin.

My brother fought for his life for three days with doctors and nurses at his side, with every worldly form of treatment they had, and on October 22, 1984, my brother flatlined.

He left his body and all the remains of loss for us to hold. I held this loss in my blood for many years, a seeping of the soul. It would visit regularly. I believed in a spiritual world, a life beyond the body. My father's lessons were not wasted on me, though it took years for them to ground, along with my own lessons slowly arriving over time.

The pain of that loss became a gift, one that I could write about, one that I can share with you now. When I set out to write a book, the true story of my life growing up in the wilderness, I was frozen inside when I came to the idea of writing about my brother. I had summoned the courage to write about everything else. It was a deep, deep wound. I feared that because of my limitations as a writer, I wouldn't be able to do the story justice. I kept working at my story, line by line and scene by scene. One evening while writing alone in my bedroom, I came to a blank space there on the page…it was the blank space in which I should write about John.

My body went into a meltdown, heavy breathing and tears swirling around inside and outside. I was in my own blizzard of emotion, though it had been twenty-five-plus years since he had died. Grief stays inside of the body, until we give it a chance to fully release. I lay on the floor of my bedroom walk-in closet, curled up in fetal position as I wept.

And in the silence, just as I had experienced all those years earlier when John left, when the truck drove up the hill that night, silence, and only the beating heart—suddenly then—I felt John's presence. He was *there,* hovering over me in my state of grief. I couldn't see his body, but he was there to the right of me, a gentle soul coming with vibrant colors. I watched the colors: reds, purples, oranges, all mixed together with John right in the center of the swirling colors.

I'm over here, he said. *I'm okay, Chloe. It's different where I am.*

I heard the words through a spiritual inner voice. Startled but not afraid, I sat up to listen to this experience. I opened my mouth to speak and tears poured again.

"I'm just so terrified to write about you! I'm just so terrified," I said out loud.

The colors were now in stillness and a voice, ever so calm, responded.

I'm in a different place now…this is about you. Write whatever you want about me, and I will be proud of you.

I lay there and wept watching my brother's spirit leave, along with the magnificent colors he brought with him.

From that moment on, I learned to write my way through the pain, opening my heart to the spiritual world, to life after death, to the miracles that await us every day if we can be opened.

I sit here writing this now, in the month of October. It's one week from the anniversary of my brother's passing. I have learned to love October; it's my favorite time of year. I've learned there is no blizzard I cannot get though, and beyond the blizzards of life come the joy, the deep richness of love, and the understanding that death is not the final chorus.

Chloe Rachel Gallaway is the author of *The Soulful Child: Twelve Years in the Wilderness,* an intuitive writing coach, and the founder of The Winged River Writer writing services. Her book is making a global impact, spreading throughout the US, the UK, and Canada. As a Intuitive Writing Coach and facilitator of the writing process, Chloe combines her experience of growing up immersed in nature with her training in mindfulness tools and literary-based writing techniques to deliver a powerful process of self-transformation and empowerment through writing. She is making a worldwide impact inspiring others write their story. Leading the VOICES book series™ movement, she is helping women, men, and youth to move from fear to courage and brave it all to share their message. For information about her programs and retreats, visit ChloeRachelGallaway.com.

Doilies

Anita Biers

I was thirty-three when my mother died, but I often feel she is still with me, seeing my life, my problems, and my hopes. Every once in a while I think she still tries to tell me something. I realized this one particular afternoon twenty-four years after Mom had been gone and I was struggling to get a new grip on life.

I had been living alone for several years when lightning struck my mobile home and burned it to the ground. The fire destroyed everything except for some books and a cedar chest full of picture albums. Fortunately, my kind landlord replaced the mobile home, and after I received a check from the insurance company, I started buying a few things to furnish it.

Prior to that day I bought some items at a second-hand store in town. Among them were some delicate, cream-colored doilies. Mom had always used doilies on furniture when I was growing up, so it was second nature for me to want to replace what had been destroyed. I bought several of them: one large square and four smaller squares.

Feeling displaced and depressed after the fire on this particular afternoon, I decided to shake it off by going shopping. Before leaving the house I placed the doilies where I wanted them. The large one went on the top shelf of a bookcase. I arranged it so the lace of a straight edge overhung the shelf. On it I placed a figurine of a Southwest adobe house. Three smaller squares went on three lower shelves and were topped with photographs. I placed the last doily on a small antique stand by the back door. On the square, I centered a five-by-seven photo of my mom, dad and my daughter taken during our last Easter together. Light poured in through the door's glass window and cheered me. I stepped back and admired my arrangement. Satisfied, I left the house.

When I returned a few hours later, I was immediately taken aback. The large doily beneath the adobe house on the bookcase's top shelf had been moved! It was now rotated to a triangular position so that a point of lace hung neatly over the shelf. It was as if someone had come in and rearranged it. The doilies on the lower shelves remained as I had left them. Perplexed, I went through the hallway and saw that the doily under my family photo on the little stand by the door had also been turned.

No one else had been in my house. No one else would have known that my mom always hung her doilies that way.

Feeling good that she was letting me know she was with me, I whispered, "Okay, Mom." Then I rearranged the last three doilies.

To this day the doilies remain arranged in that triangular way. Actually, they do look much nicer. I know I have Mom to thank for that.

Editor's Note: Anita Biers contacted me through my website. When I emailed her, we discovered that we lived relatively close to each other and decided to meet for lunch. I was immediately struck by this woman's authenticity and strength. A single mom, she has worked hard to provide for her daughter and herself. Now retired from civil service employment, Anita enjoys writing essays and stories, charcoal drawing, and hiking "roads less traveled."

Mystical Signposts

Suzanne O'Rourke

I like to think of coincidences as *signposts*. Sometimes they point you in a direction that's right for you—and maybe for somebody else as well.

Back in 1979 as I was entering my last year of college, my girlfriend Doreen and I decided to go down to Fanny Ann's, a watering hole where a fun crowd of people our age liked to gather. Fanny's, in historic Old Sacramento, was a dimly lit bar with a Gold Rush theme.

Doreen picked me up in her truck. When we arrived at Fanny's parking lot, I removed my unattractive coke-bottle glasses. Knowing that I'd been technically blind all my life with 20/2000 vision, Doreen reacted with surprise.

"What are you doing?" she asked.

"I'll be fine once we're inside," I said. "I just don't want to wear these tonight."

She shook her head and shrugged her shoulders.

We entered the dimly lit club where Gold Rush-era antiques hung from the ceiling. Old wooden booths surrounded a small dance area, and jukebox music rocked the room. Taking seats at the bar, Doreen and I ordered beers. As we sipped our beers and enjoyed the music, we chatted with the bartender and a few patrons.

Soon Doreen wandered off to join some friends. I looked around and thought I recognized two acquaintances sitting in a booth. They were the guys who had taken over the last house

I rented and had let me leave some of my belongings in the basement storage area. I remembered that one of them was named Steve. Seeing me peer at them, they waved me over.

I moved into to the old wooden booth and sat next to Steve. He re-introduced me to Mark, and they ordered me a beer. I asked Steve how my stuff in storage was doing. Did he know if my record collection was staying dry? He kind of laughed and said he thought it was fine.

Conversation flowed. The three of us easily exchanged stories and funny jokes. I was quite comfortable with Steve. He was quick with a smile and seemed to enjoy laughing out loud. After about an hour and a half, Doreen came by asking if I wanted to go home with her. Steve asked where I lived. When I told him, he said he lived in the same direction and would be happy to take me home.

It wasn't until after Doreen left that I connected the dots. Steve did not live in my direction if he was still living in my old rental. He and his buddy were not who I thought they were! I leaned in really close and said, "Who the heck are you?"

When they finally reigned in their laughter, they introduced themselves. "Steve's" real name was John O'Rourke, and Mark was actually Mark O'Rourke, John's brother. Realizing I was with strangers troubled me, especially since I was depending on them for a ride home. They saw the flash of concern.

John (*Steve*) reassured me saying, "Don't worry, I'll get you home safely."

The compassionate look in his eyes and the sincere manner with which he spoke convinced me that I was safe with him.

As it turned out, both John and Mark were traveling on motorcycles. Fortunately, I had no problem riding backseat on a bike. Mark said goodnight and headed home in a different direction from the one John and I were going.

When we arrived at my place, both of us were quite surprised to discover that John lived right across the street from me! Not only that, his dog, Angie, and I were best friends! She and I had been spending afternoons together for months.

From that night to this, John O'Rourke has been my best

friend, my love and my partner for life. We have been inseparable. Tracing our pasts, we discovered that many signposts had marked our journeys to that place and time when we first met.

Five years earlier both John and I had arrived during the *same* week to live in the *same* neighborhood in Sacramento, California. I'd come from Singapore with my brother to attend college. John had come from Pennsylvania with his girlfriend to find jobs. Over time, my brother went his own way; John and his girlfriend parted as friends.

During the next five years, both John and I, respectively, moved eight times within the area of Sacramento. Remarkably, each of us moved during the *same* week to the *same* neighborhood. I was moving into college dorms, shared houses, apartments with roommates, and finally into my own apartment. John was moving from one temporary job to the next and so on, gathering work experience. At each location we lived *less than one block* from each other. One of those moves actually put us in the *same* Victorian boarding house! I rented the converted porch studio while John lived over the garage.

John and I were both twenty-two when we started our lives together. We moved to Laguna Beach and, while living in a camper with Angie and two additional puppies for a year, started a screen printing business.

A year later we bought our first boat, a 1929 wooden powerboat. It was a leaking wreck, which we eventually restored to become a National Historic Vessel. We grew our Screen Printing Fine Art business from nothing and sold it ten years later. Then we bought, outfitted and supplied a large boat with living quarters, which we named "The Blew Moon." Shortly thereafter we set sail on the Pacific to follow our dreams.

Over the years we lived many of those dreams, sailing 10,000 miles, traveling to over forty countries, living on islands, living in other countries, and working together wherever we went.

We owned a solar company in Mexico until a drug lord told us to leave or die.

We worked as disaster inspectors for FEMA.

We built homes.

We owned a yacht brokerage.

We ran a corporate IT office in Ireland.

Now we work full time from our RV as we travel and run our international training business.

John and I have been best friends, lovers, business partners, nurturers, counselors, traveling companions and gypsy partners in life, together facing challenges all along the way.

John was dragged a mile and a half under a car, I had cancer, pirates attacked us twice, and we have been arrested in foreign countries. A few years ago John underwent heart surgery. Regardless, we feel invincible together and wouldn't want to live any other way.

Looking back, we marvel at the unseen forces that finally succeeded in bringing us together. We agree that something bigger than both of us was working to make it happen. Now, thirty-eight years later, we are happily grateful for the many *mystical signposts* that led us to that fortuitous night when love was "blind."

Editor's Note: **Suzanne and John O'Rourke** are two very special people to me. John was my student during my first year of teaching. We've kept in touch all these years. I have loved these two for as long as I've known them and have been privileged to follow the many adventures in their amazing lives.

A Picture of Susie

Beth Emeterio

My "interlude" happened with my dear friend, Susie. She was the one I called if something cool happened and I wanted to tell somebody about it. Susie was at the top of the invite list when I thought of a neat trip to take—and she was usually game. She was that kind of friend. This experience happened after Susie's death.

We met at Emory University in Atlanta when I worked as Head Athletic Trainer. Susie needed students to earn her teaching credential for SCUBA diving. Adventurous twenty-eight year old that I was, I volunteered. Eventually I earned the Dive Master Certification, and later, Susie paid my expenses on dive trips so I could assist her with students on their certification dives. It was a great system!

We shared good times and many laughs on diving trips and sometimes on jaunts to places of interest. We even took our moms on trips to Europe and Mexico. After four years I left Emory, and later Susie moved to her native state of Florida, but we remained close friends.

In 2001, she bought a small beachfront condo that was built in the fifties. I visited her twice. The place was small, uncluttered, and tastefully decorated with interesting artisan items. She loved fixing it up and took pleasure in adapting the place to her needs and preferences. The last time I was there, Susie said she was planning to remodel the bathroom by replacing the tub with a walk-in shower.

In early February 2003, several months after my second visit,

I got a call from Susie's business partner, Al. He gave me the sad news that my friend had been diagnosed with a brain tumor. She was undergoing further tests to determine if it was treatable.

The tumor turned out to be a fatal glioblastoma. Susie returned to Atlanta to receive both traditional and experimental treatments at the Emory University Hospital. I visited her a few times, and on Memorial Day weekend, a friend drove her to the Tennessee Smoky Mountains, four hours away, to visit me.

The physical changes to my always-fit friend were shocking! Although she was obviously in extreme distress from the ravages of her condition and regimens of chemo and steroids, she was still her sweet self. We had a great two-day visit, both of us knowing it would be our last on this side of heaven.

We took a ride through the Cades Cove area of the Smoky Mountains and had a picnic along a stream. We didn't talk about cancer because I knew how she must have felt about people asking unending questions about her condition. So we mostly talked about the adventures we'd go on when she felt better (even though we both knew full well that wasn't in the cards) and how much we loved *my* mountains and *her* beach.

On Sunday morning she had two episodes of ominous, debilitating pain, which caused us to leave church early. On Monday afternoon, Susie returned to Atlanta with her friend. Two weeks later, on Friday, June 13th, Susie died. I cried myself to sleep that night.

Two nights later while I was asleep—I think—Susie popped into my room! It wasn't really my room, but I was there with Susie. She was wearing something white, and she was *alive!* Not only that, she was completely well, and very *real!*

I exclaimed, "Oh my gosh, Susie, you look amazing!"

"I know!" she said, smiling, "Look at my hair!"

The last I had seen her, she had almost no hair, and her face was bloated from the medications. But now her face was back to the thin, healthy, normal "Susie," and her long blonde hair was full and thick. Playfully, I ran my hand through it to kind of fluff it or mess it up.

Then I realized that we were standing in a kind of bathroom.

Everything, from top to bottom was white, with one exception. A picture, brightly colored in shades of blue, green, pink, orange, and yellow appeared in an unusual place. It was on the wall behind and above the shower. I couldn't make out the picture, but it was conspicuously high on that wall. That is all I recall about my vision or dream or whatever it was. (I now refer to it as a mystical interlude.)

A few weeks later, Susie's memorial service was held on the beach in front of her condo. Her ashes were spread about 100 yards out in the ocean. People drifted in and out of her place all day. I told Susie's business partner about my "dream" and described in detail what I saw. I said I wanted to see the bathroom because I knew Susie had replaced the tub with a walk-in shower, but I had no idea what it looked like.

He broke into a smile and said, "Wait till you see this!"

We walked into an all-white space! Ceiling, floor, fixtures, cabinetry were all white. It was white from top to bottom, with one exception. At the back of the white shower stall, Susie had hand painted about twelve or sixteen individual four-by-four inch square tiles and composed them into an ocean mural around which she had placed a border. I recognized the bright colors from my *dream* or *vision!* I had never been there before, and Susie had not talked about it.

I exclaimed to Al, "This is what I saw!"

He answered, "I'm glad Susie came to you."

I'm glad she did, too! Seeing her healthy and smiling made me happy. I have tremendous hope that we will meet again someday.

Editor's Note: I've known Beth for decades. Her mother and I taught together at McGuffey High School, where Beth was involved in several of the plays I directed. In more recent years, Beth has settled in the Smoky Mountains of East Tennessee and makes her living as an Athletic Trainer working for a county hospital. Her hobbies include volunteering with senior citizens, hiking, camping, kayaking, working on antique cars, and until recently, beekeeping. Well known for her sharp wit and sense of humor, Beth is a welcome guest everywhere she travels.

Two Become One

Penelope Love

* * *

1992

"ATTENTION!" Mr. Mack's military command sliced through the air, dissolving all chatter in the Coral Springs High School hallway adjacent to a trophy case lining the cafeteria entrance. "Form your lines!" he ordered.

My heart pounded as sweat dripped beneath my starched-stiff polyester uniform, foreshadowing the intense Florida heat awaiting us outdoors. I'd tooted countless breaths, arranged my spindly fingers in innumerable positions, and marched a million steps to arrive precisely at this point in space-time. It was my junior year, and I was *the* chick with the pic—the piccolo, that is. I was the section leader of the mighty flutes.

Another bead of sweat fell, then... electric silence as I awaited the next marching order.

"Flutes! Here!" Mr. Mack pointed to the exact spot I should stand. "Face the wall!"

But this was no ordinary spot on the wall. His order had placed me and the entire flute brigade before the honorary historical portraits of our school's All-American athletes.

At eye level before me hung the photograph of a handsome 1981 All-American soccer player. One step left, it would have been a baseball player—or to the right, a basketball star. One step in either direction would have changed my destiny. I'd been ordered to stare at this precise spot, home to this young man's fading photograph. I never took note of his name, so captivated was I by the cheerful glint in his light-brown eyes, the confident curve of his smile, the '80s-style shortness of his blue soccer shorts, and the sheer size of his muscular thighs, but I digress. Of course, I focused mainly on his eyes.

What a nice boyfriend he'd have been, had I been around back then. My heart fluttered, then sunk in a sea of star-crossed fate. *I mean, he's pretty hot, for the '80s.* I fantasized, imagining what his whisper sounded like. What his lips tasted like. What his arm would have felt like around my shoulder, holding me close at the movies or strolling along the beach. *In the '80s we'd probably have been at a drive-in, and then what would have hap—*

"Atten-hut!" Mr. Mack snapped me back into the '90s. It was time to make our season debut.

Week after week, the band played on... but I would never be the same.

* * *

2004

"ATTENTION," the guru explained, "is one subtle non-step away from awareness of being."

It was my first meditation class, where one hour of seated practice was followed by a contemplative Q&A session. I'd chosen to attend this particular course in Hillsboro Beach, Florida, twenty miles due east of my hometown of Coral Springs, to help myself heal from a divorce and cope with the stress of my burgeoning publishing career that was draining me of all the joy of my twenties. A family crisis had drawn me back to Florida from where I'd been working tirelessly to build a new life in Princeton, New Jersey. The daily regimen of playing a musical instrument had long been abandoned and now I needed some other way to reconnect with discipline and focus.

While I liked the idea of sitting still and practicing this mental yoga, unfortunately I had no idea what the teacher was talking about. So I raised my hand, and after a brief pause that felt like forever, he called on me to speak.

"I don't understand the difference," I said with a sigh of defeat.

"In attention, there is literally *a tension* between *what you perceive to be 'you'* and the object of focus," he said, pausing and patiently waiting for the ping. "In awareness, or noticing, the sense that *you* are doing the focusing is absent—the appearance of tension dissolves and there is only awareness of What Is." He glanced into my eyes as if to ensure the words had penetrated.

But wait! Where had I seen those eyes before?

Spending the rest of class trying to figure that out, I reached only a quivering state of non-transcendence filled with *a tension*.

I just couldn't remember.

* * *

Four Nights Later

"WOULD YOU PAY ATTENTION?!" I shouted. "Oh my *Gawd!*"

My nerves were strung so high, my latent Long Island accent slipped out, revealing my roots as a native New Yorker posing as a laid-back Floridian. It was our first date and I did not like how this "meditation" teacher was driving my little Ford Probe—my precious worldly symbol of freedom that I was still pretty attached to.

He had offered to whisk me away with his own set of wheels, but I was too freaked out to brave his Honda Rebel, having once vowed to my mother that reading *Zen and the Art of Motorcycle Maintenance* was as close as I'd get to a hot-roddin' hog. I could not believe I'd accepted a date with the teacher I'd met just four nights ago. *Wasn't that supposed to be forbidden, dating a guru?!*

"Relax," he said, gently placing his hand on my knee. My whole body melted and suddenly the girl who could hardly stop talking was rendered speechless.

I don't remember where we went that night—if we'd gone out to eat, or to the movies, or someplace else. I only remember this conversation we had walking back to my bachelorette pad between the time he dropped me off and revved his way home.

"I've seen you before," he said, "at Coral Springs High School."

Good effort at a pick-up line, dude, I thought, *but it's not going to work.*

"Ummm, but I already told you I went there so how can I believe you?" I inquired with five bats of my eyelashes, my inner romantic desperate to believe it was true.

"You were leaning over the water fountain outside the gym," he continued without flinching or looking down and to the right.

Questions filled my brain. *Is he for real? Anyone could have taken a sip from that—*

"In 1993, I was there to coach at a wrestling tournament..."

Getting warmer, I mused. *He does actually know the name of the stud wrestler from that year.*

He placed his arm around me and pulled me close. "You were wearing blue gym shorts and flipping your long brown hair out of your face, and out the water fountain..."

Okay, yes. I had much longer hair at that time and he couldn't have known that from just seeing me now, I reasoned before doubt kicked in again. *But all of our shorts were blue, school colors.*

"...and you were toting a flute!"

I froze in my tracks. *OMG, I had not told him that. He was there! There is just no way he could have known.* I smiled as the jigsaw pieces of history started falling into place. Yes, the brunette bent over the water fountain and sporting blue shorts could have been someone else, but the flute was the detail that wiggled him off the hook.

"You were radiant. I know because I couldn't stop looking at you! I actually wanted to approach you then, however the age difference would have clearly been taboo..."

As my jaw dropped to the floor, God placed a question on my tongue that I'd have never otherwise thought to ask. "Wait, did you play soccer for Coral Springs High in 1981?"

His lips turned a smile my soul instantly recognized. For the first time in my life, I felt no need to fill up silence. I knew his eyes, his touch, his lips, his whisper. They were just as I had imagined. *Gulp!* My heart flooded with the same butterflies as when I first saw his photo in the hallway.

"*Now* do I have your attention?"

I replied, "Yes... you do."

Two weeks later, those words became "I do."

And we've rarely spent a day apart since that fateful night fourteen years ago.

Penelope Love, MA, a writer and publisher, is the author of the spiritual memoir *Wake Up in Love.* She publishes a vast selection of books at Citrine Publishing and coordinates programs at a spiritual training center in the Blue Ridge Mountains of North Carolina. An advocate for true love, she inspires with her *Words to Love By* blog. Come say hello! www.PenelopeLove.com

Keeping Moral

Bob Senko

I am a retired single man who has devoted most of my life to building my businesses. Although I have had many female friends and a few live-in partners, I've never married.

My parents and I remained close throughout their lives. They came from Pittsburgh to my home in Florida for two months every year at Christmastime. Both parents were with me in Florida during the last days of their lives. During a visit, Dad died suddenly from a stroke; during her visit the following year, Mom was diagnosed with pancreatic cancer. From diagnosis until her death was three weeks.

My event happened after my mother's second week in the hospital. I had been going there daily to be at her side. It was evening. The door was open a crack and light came in from the hallway. I can't remember if she was in a coma or not. I do recall that I was totally exhausted. I hadn't been able to sleep or eat much since she had been admitted. I sat in silence, looking out the window. I was not asleep.

As I gazed out the window, a voice came into my head. It said, "Would you like to know how it feels where she's going?"

At first I ignored it, thinking I'm so out of it! I need to get some sleep.

The voice spoke again. *"Would you like to know how it feels where she's going?*

I said, *Who is talking to me?*

He said, *"I'm what you call your 'guardian angel.'"*

Really? I said, not knowing whether to be amused or afraid. *So what's your name?*

"*My name is Moral,*" he answered.

I wondered, *Am I talking to myself? Am I playing a game with myself?* After a moment, I thought, *If I'm talking to myself, why would I pretend to be my guardian angel? Where would I come up with a name like MORAL? I've never heard of such a name. If I were to name my guardian angel, I'd pick something like Michael, or Gabriel, or Thomas.*

Okay, okay, I said, *so your name is Moral. But if you're my guardian angel, why have you waited until now to finally say something to me?* This is where he got my attention. I knew I was exhausted . . . still, his answer threw me!

"*I've been talking to you all your life, but you haven't listened to me since you were a child.*"

I was dumbstruck. Then he repeated, "*Would you like to know what it feels like where your mother is going?*"

Thinking I had nothing to lose, I simply said, *Yeah.*

He said, "*I'm going to let you know what it feels like where she is going.*"

In the next moment a feeling of—let's say happiness, or euphoria—I mean there's not a word in human vocabulary to explain it—overwhelmed me! Nothing can describe that awesome feeling. All I know is that when I got a grip on my emotions, I was sitting in the chair staring out the window. Then I realized that I had a smile on my face! I caught myself, and looked over at Mom in the bed. I sat there smiling, yet feeling guilty because I knew my mother was dying. But I was filled with happiness!

I went home filled with that wondrous bliss. My brother Bill was staying at my house. I didn't want to say anything to him about what I was feeling. *What would I say? How could I explain what had happened to me? How could I even begin to describe what I was feeling?* Trying to conceal it took hard work.

The bliss stayed with me for two days. On the third day as I was walked down the hall of the hospital the euphoria was beginning to wear off and tears started down my face.

I said, *Moral.*

He answered. "Yes."

Can I have that feeling again?

He said, *"I will allow you to feel it one more time, but afterwards you will not experience it again until you cross over."*

Okay.

I leaned against the wall in the hallway and sort of squatted down. The amazing bliss came back. I looked around and realized, gratefully, what had happened. Within a day or two, my mother passed serenely.

Moral has been with me since that time. I have been able to communicate with him when needed. Sometimes long periods of time go by between contacts because my head gets caught up in my businesses and affairs of life.

Once in a while, I ask, *Moral, Are you there?*

He always answers, *"Yes."*

When times get rough, Moral is always there to calm me by reminding me of God's love and his love for me.

Bob Senko is a single, professional man enjoying a solitary life in Florida. He dedicated his working years to creating and building fitness centers and spas. He now spends his time fighting for animal rights, reading, working out, traveling, and meditating on God's word.

Dreadful May Day

Lilly Kauffman

Walking home from high school on a perfectly sunny May Monday, I felt relaxed contemplating the countdown of my junior year. The work of decorating for the senior prom was over and most of the academic heavy lifting (term papers and projects) checked off. I easily crossed the main road to my quiet neighborhood street. A few more blocks to home—third house on the left—where it seemed my mother would always be waiting and glad to see her only child. Typically this time of year, we would review our day over some freshly brewed iced tea.

So far this day was like my others. I stepped onto our front porch, but as I reached for the door, an overwhelming feeling traveled through my body, a feeling I can best describe as fear and dread and unlike anything I ever experienced. Instantly my body was on high alert and my mind had no time to catch up. I had no idea what I would face inside, but did sense that it would not be people with balloons yelling "Surprise!" I felt physically weak as I turned the doorknob and crossed the threshold. Looking across the living room I saw my mother face down on the sofa sobbing uncontrollably. "Mom, Mom, what's the matter?" I begged, as books dropped and I tore toward her.

She choked out the words that her brother was dead! She was wailing now and hugging me too tightly. Her brother was big and strong and forty-nine years old. *How could this happen?* He and my aunt were away on vacation—this news a total shock.

I didn't see my uncle that often, but knew like I knew my own name that he meant everything to my mother and her family of origin. Salvatore was the firstborn of Italian immigrants and their only son. He worked hard to lift the family out of poverty, even lying at age thirteen to obtain a license to begin his first job driving a coal truck. By age forty he owned a construction company worth over a million. Many times he gave my mother blood when she was critically ill and needed direct emergency transfusions. As his given name translates, he was, to his parents and three sisters, the "savior" of the family.

The cliché "a picture of health" was chanted ceaselessly (in English and Italian) in those days following. The term "aneurysm" in ink on the death certificate did little to satisfy the "why" and bewilderment and grief of my grandparents and their daughters.

In the months of aftershocks, I witnessed a profound change in my mother and in myself. The dynamic shifted and I became the more mature one as my mother sank into a deep depression, at times inconsolable. I modeled strength and self-control, adopting a stoic Jackie Kennedy-like attitude. I would call from the payphone at lunchtime to check on her and go directly home after school to make sure she was okay. Finally, I confronted my mother with the fact that my father and I were still alive and needed her to focus on us more than her brother's death.

I've often thought how that horrible feeling on the porch that May day warned, if not prepared me for what was to come. I could have used such a dramatic signal of impending trouble other times in my life, but it has not happened since.

Lilly Kauffman, a former librarian and elementary teacher, enjoys writing essays, both serious and humorous. She is an active church volunteer engaging in pro-life work and also coordinating an ongoing project to clothe orphans in Haiti. When submitting this story, Lilly related that her faith sustains her through life's challenges. She added, "I am not surprised that these mystical experiences occur. We are, after all, spiritual beings with bodies."

The Cullen Interludes

Cara and Michael Cullen

Editor's Note: Cara, from Pittsburgh, was working for a company in Detroit. About a block from her workplace stood The Tandem Bar and Grill, a popular restaurant owned by Michael, his twin brother, John, and other investors. The Tandem was the place where Cara and Mike first met. Their journey from there to the altar encountered several mystical turns.

CARA

THE COMPANY I WORKED FOR in Detroit was located near Michael's restaurant. A few times a week, some of our work gang went there at the end of the day for drinks and dinner. Michael was usually there. His wit, sense of humor, and sunny disposition endeared him to our group. After a while, he felt like one of our gang. Even while I was dating another person, I felt attracted to Michael. I knew he was also unavailable. He didn't hide the fact that he was in a relationship.

A few years flew by quickly. Even though I was happy with my job and my life, there was nothing solid to keep me in Detroit. Yes, I had made good friends and enjoyed great times, but my roots were in Pittsburgh. When a job offer came from my hometown, I packed my bags and moved back to the *Burgh*. Living with my sister until I could find a place of my own, I dug right in on my new job and picked up with old friends as though we hadn't been separated by a minute. Soon after getting settled into my new job, I received an email from Mike.

I happily responded to his friendly, "Hi Cara, How are things going with you in Pittsburgh?" Before long we were exchanging light, amusing emails on a daily basis. I found myself looking forward to them each day. The tone of his emails indicated his interest in me. Then I learned, sadly, that he was still in the same relationship as before. Knowing how I felt about him, I decided to back away before the situation became too painful. Biting the bullet, so to speak, I asked him not to contact me while he was seeing somebody else. I needed to move forward in my life.

MIKE

IT HAD BEEN QUITE A WHILE since Cara had responded to any of my emails. I finally was set to give in to the fact that she was gone… but just one more email: "Are you ever going to talk to me again?"

She responded, asking how I was, how everyone else in Detroit was, and how things were going for me in my relationship.

I stated that the relationship was over.

Cara responded, "Well, I just started dating someone." She let that marinate for a while

I felt terrible. I had missed my chance! I needed to get my act together.

Then, after what seemed like forever, she sent a message stating, "But, I'm counting his flaws as I speak."

I'm not sure if she decided to stop seeing that person *before* we communicated but he was jettisoned back into the single scene. (She must have been captivated by my awesomeness.)

CARA

THIS IS TRUE. And it didn't take me long to break up with the other guy (like, I called him that night!). When we met for coffee, I told him that we needed to break up because a guy from Michigan had contacted me and I was pretty sure that he was "the one." I needed to pursue the relationship. I apologized for any hurt feelings and assured him it was the right thing to do. I felt happy and excited for what the future could hold.

MIKE

LET ME BACK UP A MINUTE. When Cara was coming to the Tandem we became good friends. One night, while our group was having a good time, I challenged her to a foot race in our restaurant's parking lot. I told her she likely wouldn't win because I was wearing my "fast, fast" shoes. Fortunately I beat her and, and after the race I remember putting my arm around her shoulder and having the extraordinary feeling that we fit together. It was always a joy seeing her come into the restaurant.

When Cara moved back to Pittsburgh, we had a talk about us and my situation before she left. I was confused and torn between my then-current situation and my feelings for Cara. The woman I was with at the time had a son from a previous relationship. I had been helping raise him for a number of years. Even though the romantic feelings once shared between his mother and me were all but gone, I felt an obligation to him, even at my own unhappiness. It was very difficult knowing that the woman I felt a special bond with and loved was leaving Detroit.

This situation caused me to do some serious soul-searching. I thought back to how my current relationship began. The woman I was with had been a single mom living with her dad and looking for a way out. She and I became good friends. We had similar interests and enjoyed doing things together, so we decided to share a home. Unfortunately our relationship did not grow during our time together. Eventually we came to that realization and went our separate ways.

I questioned if I had ever been in love with her. Did I have an unrealistic view of what love is? I knew I had not experienced the sense of what *I* felt love should be and I questioned if I would ever really know love.

All these questions were with me when Cara and I started dating long distance. One of us flew to Pittsburgh or Detroit over weekends, we emailed often, and we talked on the phone for at least an hour every evening. It was great! I felt alive!

There is value in long-distance dating. Multiple emails and long telephone conversations bring two people together. So often when you go out together, conversations only scratch the surface or they're interrupted and brief. It's important for a couple to be able to enjoy each other conversationally. I would intently listen as she described her day and what she was doing, feeling as though I were right there with her. Spending an hour on the phone each day is a great litmus test for compatibility. I was already smitten with Cara, but those phone conversations sealed the deal for me. I was falling in love, the kind of love I always searched for and could share.

First Mystical Interlude

CARA

OUR FIRST MYSTICAL INTERLUDE occurred in Cleveland on a cold day in October of 2000. Michael and I had been dating for a few months. My friend Cindy and I met in Cleveland to attend a weekend social event. Michael drove in from Detroit to join us.

On the morning we were returning home, Michael and I stood in the cold waiting for the valet to bring my car from the parking garage. We shivered with our hands sunk into coat pockets as we made idle chitchat.

Smiling, Michael said, "You'll never guess what I found in my pocket."

I guessed an old gum wrapped in paper, a small shoe horn, a rubber band, and other unusual items while thinking to myself, *I can play this game. He'll never guess what I have in my pocket.*

He opened his hand to reveal a tiny bulb from a string of Christmas lights. I started to giggle and exclaimed, "You'll never guess what's in my pocket!"

I brought out an *identical* bulb!
We broke into laughter.
Go figure!

Second Mystical Interlude

MIKE

SO HERE I AM, hopelessly in love. We gathered a bus load of our restaurant patrons and we were off on a birthday celebration for Cara and a pub crawl in Detroit. At the end of the tour, steeled by the days events and perhaps a Guinness or two, I got down on a knee in the bus and I asked Cara to marry me. She was a bit taken aback, rightfully so, and her words were caught in her throat.

It was then that my brother John yelled, "Where's the hardware? You can't ask someone to marry you if you don't have the hardware!"

She had her reprieve, "Yeah, where's the hardware, you can't ask me to marry you without the hardware."

Months later I had made arrangements to buy an engagement ring for Cara. On the drive to pick it up, my mind started going in circles. I was thirty-six. As I stated previously, I had questions about love. I began to wonder if I were doing the right thing. Was marriage for me? Even though it felt right in my heart, I knew that marriage would be a major life change. I knew that I was in love with Cara and she was in love with me. I wanted it to last forever.

I called on my mom, who had passed years before. In my mind I said, *Please, Mom, give me a sign if this is the right thing to do.*

At that moment driving on interstate 696, I came up over a hill facing an overpass across which rolled a huge red truck with four-foot letters spelling out the name:

RIZZO

When I saw that, it was like a two-by-four to the head. Cara's last name was Rizzo.

Mom's answer!

Third Mystical Interlude

CARA

AFTER WE WERE ENGAGED, we flew back and forth between Pittsburgh and Detroit frequently on weekends. Checking in at the gate at Pittsburgh Airport one day, I learned that my flight had been canceled. Everybody was being rerouted onto a different plane, which meant that we had to stand in a long line for re-ticketing. Folks in the line chatted, complaining about the situation. I got into a conversation with a woman standing nearby. We both got our tickets and went our separate ways.

Knowing I had at least two hours to kill, I went into a café and sat at a table. The woman I had talked with came in a few minutes later. Seeing me, she came over and sat down to resume our conversation.

We sat and talked for at least an hour about our jobs, our families, and so forth until I got around to telling her that my fiancé owned a bar in Detroit.

"Oh, where is it located?" she asked, "What's it called?"

"It's the Tandem Bar and Grill," I answered.

"Oh, I know the Tandem! I have been there a number of times. Well then you must know Uncle Bill!"

"Yes, I do know Uncle Bill!" I exclaimed, thinking she was referring to a perennial patron at Michael's bar who bore that nickname. "How do you know Uncle Bill?"

"He's my brother-in-law."

I was incredulous because of the age difference between the two. Uncle Bill was an elderly gentlemen. "I don't think he's the same person I know," I said.

"Yes," she insisted, "you know, Billy, ... Bill Rohr."

"Bill Rohr? He's going to be *my* brother-in-law!" I blurted. "He's married to Mike's sister, Laura!"

So, it turned out that I was with my brother-in-law's sister-in-law. Her husband, Danny, and Bill Rohr are brothers.

What makes this mystical interlude even more mystical is the fact that she, Jan, never expected to be at the Pittsburgh airport that day. She had boarded a direct flight from Memphis, Tennessee, to Detroit, Michigan. The plane had been rerouted through Pittsburgh for some reason. Out of all those people lined up for tickets, she and I became acquainted!

I can't explain what made these things happen.

But happen, they did.

Mike and I are grateful.

The Cullens from Michigan have been happily married for fifteen years. They are the proud parents of two daughters, Mary Kate and Allison Joan.

Answers from Another Place and Time

Beverley Golden

Throughout my life, I've sometimes learned the hard way that there aren't always answers to the questions we have. And then sometimes, quite magically, the answers present themselves in the most unexpected of ways. This story is about one of those questions and the unusual way the answer appeared.

When my daughter Lani was seven, we had a most interesting, almost unexplainable experience with a past-life regression. The precipitating event happened rather innocently. We were all excited about a birthday celebration, especially Lani, as it was for the parent of one of her closest school friends and she was excited to hang out with him outside of school. Lani was an outgoing and extremely likeable child, a little bit precocious too, and she was eager to be the one to share our plans with our next door neighbor, who happened to be outside. As we left our house for the early evening party, Lani gleefully shouted, "We're going to a party and we're going to be home REALLY LATE!"

Someone in our wild and crazy world must have heard, because when we arrived home that night, our once-secure home had been broken into and completely ransacked. Lani was visibly shaken and couldn't get over the assault on our house, especially her room. Being in our home became extremely traumatic for her and her fear didn't subside, even as time went on. In her words, our house became "scary."

Her fear of being in our house continued, and eventually she refused to go into the basement unaccompanied. This was unsettling because her drum set was in the basement. Before the "event" she loved hanging out down there by herself and playing her drums! Even when someone was willing to join her, she avoided the basement whenever possible.

My daughter and I have always been close. To this day, we have an open and honest way of communicating. One day, weeks after the break-in, we were sitting on my bed talking. I could see there was something troubling her, something she wanted to say, but wasn't. I asked her what was going on and she looked at me quite innocently and said, and these are her exact words, "Sometimes I think you're a burglar with my mommy's face on."

What? I couldn't imagine where that idea came from. It didn't make any sense to me at the time. I continued to console her and assure her that she didn't have to be concerned. I told her I was her mommy, definitely not a burglar! This didn't seem to help. There was something going on within her and it seemed she was just not going to let go of it on her own. She eventually refused to even go into the basement, at all. We needed to do something, as so far nothing had worked to alleviate her fears.

The time was the mid-80s. Our very progressive doctor suggested something that might have seemed far out to most people, but we were open to his idea of introducing us to a woman who did past-life regressions. Although I had no direct knowledge or experience of this kind of work, I was curious and always open to new things. My husband and I talked about it with Lani and explained that it might help her with her fear of being in our home. Without too many questions or hesitation, she was eager and willing to try it.

We all had deep respect for our doctor and trusted him completely. He had actually been present at Lani's premature birth. He was an important part of all of our lives since, so he was a well known presence in our family. All three of us made the decision together, feeling there wasn't too much to lose and maybe lots to gain. We might even uncover and hopefully release some of the fear my daughter was carrying—a fear that had frankly become a burden. My husband was willing to come along with us for moral support and Lani and I were ready to face whatever came up.

In our wildest imaginings, we could never have envisioned the answer we were about to get!

The woman, Charlotte, was a rather eccentric and an almost larger-than-life kind of personality. She thanked us for trusting her and told us she was a shaman and trained in multiple spiritual practices and had a lot of experience with this kind of work. Her apartment was sparse, decorated with crystals and feathers. I also remember how much light was coming into the apartment through the floor-to-ceiling windows.

After a bit of friendly conversation, she led my daughter and me to her bedroom and asked us to lie beside each other on her bed. When we were comfortable, she asked for our permission to proceed and then guided us into a kind of relaxed quasi-trance state. This was very new for both Lani and me, but somehow we felt relaxed enough to allow what was happening to happen. My husband wasn't directly involved in the process, but was sitting in a chair in the room to support us.

What did occur was immediate. Lani, Charlotte, and I all saw the exact same scene at the same time: a large, turn-of-the-century Victorian-era mansion, maybe in London. A boisterous party was in progress on the main floor of one side of the house, which was brightly lit. People were laughing and dancing. The other side of the house was dark. A young man wearing a soft-brimmed cap with an empty satchel slung over his shoulder lurked outside in the shrubbery. He quietly slipped into the house through a partly open window and crept up the narrow staircase to a second-floor bedroom, where the guests' fur coats had been placed.

He unexpectedly woke up a child who was asleep in her bedroom on the second floor. Her bedroom was beside the room where fur coats lay. As he moved past her room (presumably to steal the coats and whatever other valuables he found), he woke her up. Upon seeing the stranger's face, she screamed out in terror! Lani and I recognized that I was the young burglar lad and my daughter was the little girl he had startled! So now, "Sometimes I think you're a burglar with my mommy's face on" made perfect sense. I don't remember exactly how we felt in the moment, but we all accepted it as a past life event. If we had stopped to think about it much we might have questioned if it were real, but it was a completely believable experience for us, for we actually witnessed it together.

The fact that Lani, myself, and even Charlotte, who was facilitating the process, saw it, made it all the more powerful and credible. My sense at the time was that even Charlotte was surprised that all three of us literally saw the same scene as it unfolded. My husband was amazed and totally accepting of what had just happened, especially because our intention was to help Lani release her fear. It felt like maybe this might help.

What was most fascinating and beneficial is that it did alleviate some of Lani's fears. At least she stopped clinging to the thought that I was a burglar. I still wonder and marvel at how the three of us saw the same scene at the same time. There was no power of suggestion used. It was vivid, alive and spontaneous. Each time I write or tell the story, I am aware that it sounds somewhat beyond belief.

That scene is as alive for me today as the day we first saw it more than thirty years ago. And it still *feels* real. Lani and I rarely talk about it, but when I brought it up recently she told me she would do a past-life regression again if she had some recurring issue that she wanted to resolve. She also said she would definitely consider taking her child for one if she felt it would help, especially knowing the way it helped her.

One thing I do know is that this experience has kept me open and willing to receive answers to questions, wherever they come from. Even if those answers come from another place, in another time.

Beverley Golden lives in Toronto, Canada. She is a writer, storyteller, peacenik, and health and vitality consultant, who loves testing unconventional ways to shift paradigms in the playing fields of health and wellness, storytelling and creativity as a path to world peace. Her best-selling book, *Confessions of a Middle-Aged Hippie,* bursts with anecdotes from her years in the entertainment industry, coupled with her stories of survival from a life lived with health issues. She shares her thought-provoking observations on the *Huffington Post*. Visit her on: www.beverleygolden.com.

Birth of Gratitude

Stacey Flynn

There was a time when I thought I had my life planned out. It revolved around my little daughter, whom I loved so fiercely that sometimes I couldn't even sleep at night. The thought of separating myself from her caused me physical pain, and the idea of hers being just another little face in a sea of others when she started school truly made me cry. Although it was still almost an unbearable thought to me, I was learning to focus on what *I* might do while she was in school. *I* was going to go back to school too, and do some things *I* hadn't had time to do in the years when I had been solely focused on her—until we got the news that I was pregnant.

Without going into detail, this was not supposed to happen for medical reasons. We had been advised not to have another pregnancy, so another child was not a consideration in our plans for the future. But that's the news we got. A baby was on the way.

My husband Tommy and I approached the process with detachment knowing that chances were very slim that I would be able to carry a baby full term and give birth. Actually, that's probably a charitable description of the way we approached it. I'm not proud to admit that there were days when I prayed it would be over so I didn't have to worry about it or deal with it anymore.

As we progressed through the next several months, Tommy and I maintained our detachment from the fact that I was pregnant. That's the best way I can explain it. When we learned that we were expecting a boy, we, at least in some part, allowed ourselves to feel some excitement. One day Tommy brought home a tiny pair of work boots. Another day, while shopping, I picked up a baby blue sleeper that said "Daddy's Boy." That was it up to the point when we should have had only two months to go. That was absolutely all the preparation we did.

Looking back, I still can't fully explain the reasoning. Medically, it certainly felt like one thing after the other was stacked against us. Maybe not allowing ourselves to get too involved with the idea of an actual baby was self-preservation. Maybe we were insulating ourselves against the harsh reality that this was probably not going to end well. That's what I've told myself for years. The other thing I've told myself, and anyone else I've ever been in a position to tell, is that it was my biggest *forever* lesson that God knows what I need way more than I ever *think* I know what I need.

Fast forward to January 3, 2002. After dropping my little girl off at kindergarten for her first day back after Christmas break, I stopped at the hospital for what should have been a routine pre-natal visit. With a due date of February 26, I hadn't even reached the point of semi-weekly visits yet. Little did I know, I would not go home that day or the next or the next until more than a month later.

The routine blood pressure check set off an alarm that *something* was wrong. The something was pre-term labor— even though I couldn't feel anything! I remember being admitted and filling out paperwork as it pertained to a living will, religious preference, etc., all the while feeling that I needed to get all that out of the way and figure out who was going to pick my little girl up from school.

Things moved very quickly afterwards. I don't remember a whole lot until that night. Tommy was there with me. It seemed as if nothing the doctors and nurses were doing yielded results, so they kept increasing the intensity of the drugs they were administering to stabilize my blood pressure and stop the pre-term labor, which I still didn't feel. As the night wore on, I remember losing more and more control of my body and feeling more and more helpless.

We had a wonderfully compassionate nurse, Laura. Later, Tommy told me he overheard her in the hallway, vehemently telling another nurse, "I will NOT let them lose this baby tonight!" (He also told me he thought he was going to lose not only the baby, but me, too.)

In a strange twist of circumstances, after hours of my receiving intravenous magnesium sulfate meant to relax uterine muscles and stop contractions, my body was rendered nonfunctional, and my alarmingly high blood pressure plummeted to 60-something over 20-something. During that lowest point and before the professionals in charge realized my crisis, I experienced something l will never forget.

I had a sort of tunnel vision feeling, where suddenly the discomfort was leaving. I remember seeing a very bright light, which eventually looked the way light appears when it shines through a stained glass window. In that light, I saw a baby boy. The best way I can describe it is that it was similar to the way we typically see the Christ child depicted in a manger scene. I was at peace and unafraid. Then suddenly, I was back in my hospital room. My husband, my nurse and doctors were standing over me. I remember saying, "I just saw Jesus."

Laura exclaimed, "Honey, I'm sure you did!"

I believe that was a near-death experience. Although I must admit that the rational part of me has always wondered if it was just my mind in the face of too many drugs, in my heart, I don't think so.

That was only the first night of many nights that would be problematic. Finally, at 4:17 a.m. on January 28, 2002, our perfect baby boy was born, almost a month before his due date. They whisked him away before I heard him cry. In that moment, I knew I had never wanted anything as much as I wanted my tiny baby boy in my arms.

Today our son, Ian, is a beautiful, healthy, strong, amazing sixteen-year-old. I will never look at him and not remember how close we came to never having him at all. I never look at my son or start any day without feeling gratitude.

This experience, among others, has shown me that God

presents me with things I most want to avoid until I learn to handle things the way I *know* in my heart He wants me to handle them. Conversely, I do know He also protects me in situations where I know my heart is right.

I wonder if I am alone in an awareness of this sort of experience? I don't think so.

Stacey Flynn is a loving wife of twenty-six years and mother of a twenty-five-year-old daughter and sixteen-year-old son. She devotes her life to her family and is known as a selfless woman who goes above and beyond in everything she does. Stacey enjoys spending time at home, exercising, cooking for her family, painting, writing, reading, gardening, and boating. She encourages her children to live in the moment and believe that everything in their lives happens for a reason, just as she's seen in her own life.

Sisters Forever

Judy McDowell and Debbie Sweetie

JUDY

OUR SISTER, PAULETTE, was a lover of life. Her motto for living was two-fold: work hard and play hard. She worked hard at the detail shop, which she and her nephew owned, and she played hard, especially during her annual winter vacations on Montego Bay, Jamaica. A lover of people, partying, a glass or two of wine, or a Bombay sapphire martini, she had a favorite expression for whether or not she should tip a glass: "It's 5:00 somewhere!" Having never married, P, as everybody called Paulette, was a great companion to our mother, Anna. She was also best friend to every family member and everyone who knew her.

On Sunday morning of January 22, 2008, Paulette and our mom left home for their usual Sunday routine: to have breakfast at a restaurant near the detail shop, then stop at the shop nearby where Paulette would do a few clean-up chores. Neither of them suspected how that Sunday would end.

Shortly after my sister started her work at the shop, she suddenly fell over and started vomiting. Mom immediately called me because I lived close by. My husband, Dave, and I rushed to the shop. Paulette, in obvious pain, held the right side of her head repeating, "My head hurts...I don't know, I don't know."

I drove her to Canonsburg Hospital and my husband and Mom followed. While Paulette was undergoing a CT scan, I called our sisters, Debbie and Janice, and my grown son and daughter. The scan quickly revealed a massive brain aneurysm. Paulette was immediately life-flighted to Pittsburgh's Allegheny General Hospital. I can still see her giving us a small wave as they whisked her away.

Shortly after her arrival, she was taken into the operating room where the chief brain surgeon attempted to repair the aneurysm. Afterwards, the doctor sadly announced to our family that the aneurysm, which had been bleeding into the brain, was too massive to repair. He said Paulette would be brain dead and need a nursing home for life if she survived.

Our family was stunned by the news! We had differing opinions about what we should do for her. My sisters and I agreed that Paulette would not want to survive in a vegetative state. Others wanted to keep her alive. We recalled that she had a living will and also an organ donor card.

My sister Debbie and I were designated to get Paulette's original documents and deliver them to the hospital. We knew that important papers were kept in the family safe, located in the basement of Paulette's house. The safe was an antique, which our grandparents had brought over from Italy in the late 1800s. It weighed a ton.

As Debbie and I arrived at the house and headed downstairs, we were second-guessing ourselves about if we were doing the right thing. Little did we know that our questions would soon be answered.

Debbie, as executor of' Paulette's will, read from a slip of paper each step of the safe's combination while she slowly and carefully turned the dial. I waited somberly for the door to open. Nothing happened. Debbie started over again, this time by reading aloud each step and meticulously setting the dial in place while I watched from behind. Nothing happened. Debbie handed me the slip of paper and we tried it over again, this time with me reading each position aloud to her. Nothing happened.

Both of us were tearful. She looked up at me and said, "Let's wait for a few minutes before trying again. I think that after three times, the combination gets locked out."

Through our tears and frustration, we went into an adjoining room and started to say things like, "P, we thought this is what you want," and "P, we need those papers," and "Please open the safe." After a few moments, we returned to the room.

As we entered, both of us heard a soft click and, amazed, watched the safe's door swing open! We stood aghast at first, then fell to our knees hugging each other, crying and thanking Paulette and God! After reading through the papers, we were convinced that we were making the right decision for our beloved sister.

Delivering the documents, we learned that Paulette had to be kept alive for ten more days. Because she was initially admitted as an emergency trauma patient, the law requires that a patient must be kept alive for ten days after surgery to verify no possibility of recovery before the living will can go into effect and organs can be harvested. The surgeon offered to do another CT scan in the next few days to make certain there was no brain activity.

Meanwhile, family and friends gathered around Paulette at the hospital each day. On the fifth day after surgery, another scan was taken, showing no change. At that point, the family as a whole consented to let Paulette go. The Center for Organ Recovery and Education (CORE) was then notified to take over.

After meeting with CORE nurses, our family, still shaken from the decision we had made, went into the waiting room. I think we were still second-guessing whether we had done the right thing. Ironically, Oprah was on TV doing a show about *organ donors*. Oprah announced that she was sending donor families and recipients, both, on a free trip to *Jamaica*. That announcement resonated with all of us as a sign that we were, for sure, following Paulette's wishes. Her living will stipulated that she wanted her ashes spread in *Montego Bay, Jamaica!*

That night, after kissing my mom and family goodnight and leaving for home, I had a good feeling. I kept telling my husband that I felt at peace with the decision we had made. Well, P confirmed it, again. Entering my bedroom I saw a light going on and off in a mixture of jewelry on my dresser. It was from a pair of light-up Steeler earrings *given to me by Paulette.*

They were blinking! To me it was another confirmation that she approved.

Several days later, CORE informed us that they had recipients for a heart and pancreas. The heart could be preserved and transported for a later transplant, but the pancreas had to be transplanted within an hour after Paulette's death. The pancreas recipient would be brought to the hospital and prepared for transplant surgery and Paulette's breathing tube would be removed.

When that day came, family and friends came to say their last goodbyes. Our sister Janice took Mom home. Debbie, our husbands, and I remained. Debbie and I had arranged with CORE to be with Paulette when she took her last breath. We couldn't bear to let our sister die alone or with strangers.

Our husbands went to the waiting room while we suited up in scrubs for a sterile environment. At 3:30 p.m., we entered the operating room with the CORE team. They explained the procedure to us, then removed the breathing tube. Paulette began breathing on her own. We held her hands, prayed, and sang to her. The CORE team joined in song as we sang "Amazing Grace."

At about 4:45, the CORE team informed us that the heart and pancreas had been deprived of sufficient oxygen to be transplantable. After Paulette stopped breathing they would harvest the skin and corneas. Saying there was no longer a need to remain in the sterile environment, they invited us to accompany them as they moved Paulette to a private room.

We arrived there and were joined by our husbands. At 5:00 p.m., Paulette took her last breath. Debbie and I looked at each other and quoted Paulette, saying "It's 5:00 somewhere!"

At that moment, our four mobile phones began to ring—even though we had turned them off earlier as a hospital requirement! Astonished, we looked at each other and acknowledged that P was somehow responsible.

To this day, we *know* that the after-life is celebrating one hell of a happy hour! There, it's probably five o'clock always.

Sisters forever until we meet again.

DEBBIE

JUDY DESCRIBED THE EVENTS just as we experienced them together. I would like to add a detail to when Paulette was moved into a private room after the breathing tube was removed. We were surprised and thrilled to find that the window of that particular room overlooked the Grand Hall, a place where P spent many years as an employee.

My story picks up when we met with the funeral director, who knew our family. We asked if we could do something a little different from his usual procedure, such as bringing wine into the funeral home and having a toast in celebration of Paulette's life. He agreed, saying that people would be talking about it for years to come.

In preparation of the memorial service, we arranged photographs, flowers, and a replica of a parrot (since P was a Parrothead). At the gathering, we played Jimmy Buffett music. After prayers were spoken, everybody raised a glass of wine and shouted, "It's five o'clock somewhere!" feeling that P was among us.

Meanwhile, CORE had been able to harvest the skin and corneas. We later learned that skin used for burn victims can be preserved for up to five years. The corneas went to a fourteen-year old boy.

In May 2009, we attended CORE's annual celebration of life ceremony at their headquarters at RIDC Park in Harmarville, Pennsylvania. A few hundred of us gathered in a large garden to hear a few speakers.

As we stood there listening, our speaker asked everyone to look up at the sky. We were amazed to see what is described as a double rainbow halo, or orb. Although it was cooler than usual for May, there had been no rain that day. The speaker said she had never seen anything like it. Neither had we. We took a photograph, but the colors don't appear because of the brightness. It was just another surprising incident to associate with our beloved sister!

Paulette wanted her ashes spread in Montego Bay, Jamaica,

where she spent many winter vacations. She had even willed money to cover expenses for the trip. I will never forget Oprah's program about donors' families and recipients coincidentally playing in the hospital waiting room the day our family made the decision allowing P to pass as an organ donor.

On the one-year anniversary of her passing, my sister, Janice, my husband, Billy, and I traveled there. We found an area on the beach where the tide gently came in along some rocks and a standing tree. That is where we scattered the remains of our beloved sister, Paulette.

We wrote "Sisters Forever" in the sand.

Editor's Note: Judy is my neighbor. She and her sister Debbie came to my house one day and shared this mystical interlude. Judy, known for her sunny disposition, kind heart, and willingness to help those in need, is a popular member of our neighborhood. A loving wife, mother of two, and grandmother of four (and one grandpuppy), she is dedicated to her family.

Debbie, whom I met for the first time that day, is soft-spoken, with kind green eyes and an honest face. The youngest sister of three, Debbie is married with no children. She is a pet lover who enjoys baking, gardening, and traveling.

Lydia

Carol White

Years ago my roommate, Paula, and I were between jobs and decided to treat ourselves to a month-long vacation in San Juan, Puerto Rico. Before we left, Helene, a mutual friend of ours, gave us a few contacts. One found us a small studio apartment in a lovely neighborhood with reasonable rent. Helene also told us to be sure to contact her close friend, Sonny, who would invite us to parties and show us around the island.

After we settled into our new digs, we called Sonny. He greeted us warmly and asked if we'd like to spend the weekend with him and other friends in a large home in the rainforest. We were only too happy to oblige!

The next day, we eagerly repacked a few things, looking forward to meeting Sonny. He arrived in the morning driving an old, but serviceable, dark green Jeep. A tall, good-looking man with an even tan, sun-bleached hair, and warm brown eyes, Sonny seemed perfectly comfortable in his khaki cargo shorts and black T-shirt. Excited, we hopped into the Jeep, merrily anticipating our new adventure.

Late in the afternoon, the three of us arrived at a sprawling wood-framed house set in the middle of lush vegetation and surrounded by massive shade trees. After a brief hike through the breathtaking area, Paula and I settled into separate bedrooms, delighted and thankful to have been included in the weekend.

Later that evening, we convened for happy hour on a large deck off the living room where Sangria and snacks were served. The group was a congenial mix of a few singles and two or three married couples, all ranging in age from their twenties to early thirties. The small crowd welcomed Paula and me as if we were old friends, and immediately invited us to dance to the lively music. Much later, a tasty barbeque was prepared by Anita and George, one of the young couples sharing the weekend with us.

After the day of traveling, hiking in the bright sun, a full meal, and more wine than I was used to drinking, I felt exhausted. Excusing myself, I returned to my room. The rain hadn't yet started, but after settling into bed I heard a soft patter, which quickly turned into a downpour. It was exactly the white noise I needed to fall asleep.

It must have been about 3:00 a.m. when I was suddenly awakened.

"Get up! You must help me!"

A rain-drenched, young woman with long, dark hair was standing beside my bed. Water from her sopping hair ran over her tan London Fog raincoat and dripped onto the wooden floor.

"Help me!" she cried, in a Hispanic accent.

Startled and barely able to budge, I stared at her. "Who are you? What are you doing here?" I gasped.

"I'm Lydia!" she shrieked.

I felt as if I were trying to move through wet cement. At the same time, I knew I wasn't dreaming. The woman was standing beside my bed beseeching my help.

"This isn't my house," I explained. "I don't know what I can do to help you."

She was distraught, and went on pleading for my help. I wanted to get out of bed and alert Paula next door, but I felt too weak to move.

"Lydia, you must leave this room and find Sonny!" I ordered. "He'll be able to help you."

I must have fallen asleep while Lydia was still in my room, for I don't recall anything after that.

In the morning, while Paula remained asleep in her room, I slipped downstairs to join Sonny and his guests at the breakfast table. Every detail about the incident came back to me.

"Oh! I almost forgot," I said, between sips of much-needed coffee. "The strangest thing happened! A woman named Lydia came into my room last night…she was soaking wet and needed some kind of help. Sonny, did she find you? I'm afraid I was so out of it, I wasn't able to get up and look for you."

Sonny looked at me like I was crazy.

"What are you talking about?" he asked.

"I just told you. Lydia was in my room. I can't believe she went out in that rain! I thought maybe she'd crashed on the sofa."

Sonny stared, wide-eyed. Everybody was silent.

Feeling slightly bewildered, I asked, "Who is she?"

"Lydia is a friend of mine," Sonny said. "She owns this house. But she's in Spain right now." He gazed out the window at the trees. "No one's mentioned her since you've been here," he added. "How do you know her name?"

"She told it to me. Maybe she was annoyed because of all the people sleeping here."

"Lydia's in Spain," he repeated.

"Not anymore," I insisted. "She came here last night."

"Describe her," he said.

I gave him every last detail of her appearance: her dark wavy hair, slim figure and the rain-soaked, belted trench coat. He and others who knew Lydia sat there in shock.

Sonny scratched his head then leaned forward addressing me slowly, "Carol…if Lydia actually came here in the middle of the night, she would be here this morning." Smiling, he nodded his head, "Lydia, as I told you, is in Spain, isn't that right, George?"

"But you agree that the woman I described is your friend, Lydia." I said, perplexed. "She woke me up!"

"You were probably dreaming," George said with a gesture that indicated I should forget about it.

"I wasn't dreaming!" I insisted. "She woke me up. Besides, how do you explain the fact that I described Lydia to you, and she gave her name as Lydia?" I gestured, palms raised, "Do you think I'm making this up? I haven't noticed any photographs in this house... and not one of you has even mentioned her!"

The jovial group, doubtful of my experience, laughed and commented about the "crazy" New Yorker's tale.

"Can you imagine such a dream?" Anita said. "Carol, you're in a strange place and most likely all that wine got to you." The others agreed.

"Come on and have some breakfast with us," someone said.

Wanting to take advantage of the beautiful sunshine, Sonny suggested we change into our bathing suits for a dip in the pool. The conversation about Lydia was over.

I lost contact with Sonny after returning to the States, so wasn't able to follow up to see if he had contacted Lydia about her whereabouts during the weekend I spent at her home.

The *why* and *how* Lydia appeared at my bedside that night will always remain a mystery. That Lydia woke me up and pleaded for my help is *real*—so real that a new window to the world has opened for me.

I will always wonder why Lydia came to me that night and what her message meant. I regret that I may never know.

Carol White is an award-winning novelist, playwright, and freelance writer. Her essays and columns have been published by The Sun Sentinel, Writers Journal, Insight for Playwrights, Working Writers, Woman's World, The Florida Writer, and Senior Scene. She is a frequent fiction contributor to the East Hampton Star. She is a member of the National League of American Pen Women, South Florida Theatre League, Florida Writers Association, Florida Mystery Writers, and National Women's Book Association. She was the former Executive Producer for the Boca Raton Theatre Guild. Carol moderates playwriting and memoir workshops, and is a popular speaker at libraries and women's groups in south Florida. She can be reached via email at polowhite@aol.com or though her website www.carolwhitefiction.com.

Pennies from Heaven

Patty Kumper

In her day, Kitty Gable was a tall, slender and beautiful woman who loved living life to the fullest. A devoted mother to my sister and me, she was a selfless person who always made herself available for others. Until my dad died, Mom took little time for herself. But it should be known that she was a force to be reckoned with.

Kitty found new freedom when she was widowed at age sixty-five. She began doing things she had put on hold for years, such as reading and traveling with friends. Mom never passed up an opportunity to celebrate. In fact, I think she celebrated life in a medley of ways. For example, we were amazed during a family vacation in Puerto Rico when at age seventy-two Grandma Kitty hopped on a horse and rode the beach with the rest of us! She loved a good time, a good joke, and was always ready to laugh at herself.

Mom and I enjoyed reading the same books and discussing them. She became interested in books about life after death, so we read Brian Weiss on reincarnation and several books about near-death experiences. Two other things my mother especially loved were angels and pennies. Even though she wasn't a particularly religious person, she surrounded herself with lovely pictures and figures of angels. And when she saw a penny on the ground or in an unexpected place, she'd pick it up believing that an angel had placed it there for her to find.

Sadly, at age seventy-six my mother was diagnosed with ALS or Lou Gehrig's Disease, a cruel and unforgiving sickness. First she lost her ability to swallow. Two years later she lost her ability to speak. Until the last year of her life, Kitty communicated with us by writing. During her final year, she could only move her head to indicate yes or no.

Mom was in Pittsburgh and I lived in Richmond, Virginia. During her illness I made countless trips back and forth. When she was placed in hospice care, Kitty made it clear that she wanted to end her misery the only way available to her. She refused her feeding tube. I booked my flight.

Preparing for an extended stay in Pittsburgh, I went grocery shopping for my family. It was a cold, rainy day. I pulled into the store's parking lot and sat in silence, feeling sad and tired. After a few minutes, I slowly opened the car door, and I looked down on three pennies beside my car. The last thing I wanted to do was stoop in the pouring rain for three pennies! But I knew my mother would never approve had I not. As I picked up those cold, wet copper coins, I uttered, "Damn it, Mom!"

At her bedside in Pittsburgh, I told Mom about finding the pennies and how I'd cursed her. She delighted me by smiling and nodding her head. As family and friends poured in to say their last goodbyes, she'd turn her head toward me, prompting me to tell the story to each visitor or group.

My dear mother died within the week following my arrival. I felt deeply grateful that my story about those pennies made her smile near the end.

Two days after the funeral, my husband and I flew to Desert Palm, California, on a previously scheduled business and pleasure trip. I left home with a heavy heart. After checking into our hotel, I couldn't make myself unpack. Delaying as long as I could before imparting gloom to my husband, I reluctantly began the arduous task.

I took my time shaking things out and organizing our clothing and toiletries. At last I unzipped the final bag containing my shoes. When I raised the lid, there I discovered a shiny copper penny atop a mound of shoes! Picking it up and holding it to my chest, I cried silently. My tears were partly from grief and also from joy. I held it lovingly, knowing that Mom was reaching out to me!

From that time to this, pennies have appeared in unlikely places, often at inopportune, but appreciated times, not only for me, but also for my sister and both our families. When this happens, each of us recognizes and savors the gift, knowing that our "angel" left it for us to find.

I have always been grateful that Mom and I together read and discussed books about life after death. Somehow that experience eased her passing for both of us. It might have also opened me to recognizing those shiny, copper gifts as pennies from heaven.

Patty Kumper is living the life of the retired with the same gusto she gave to raising her family and her career. She and her husband of forty-nine years take every opportunity to spend time with family and friends. She is thrilled to have her story published knowing others might appreciate her mother's beliefs when glancing down at a penny from heaven and keeping her mother's memory alive.

Patient Precognitions

Janine Rihmland, M.D.

Editor's Note: The next two stories came from my primary care physician, Janine Rihmland. I've heard it said that your *career* is what you get *paid* for; your *calling* is what you were *made* for. Dr. Rihmland is one of those fortunate individuals whose career and calling are one in the same. When I asked if she had experienced any mystical interludes, she told me that when a patient she hasn't seen for a long period of time suddenly enters her thoughts and lingers there, that person will either show up or call within a week with a serious need. These two stories reveal the amazing outcomes that have resulted from Dr. Rihmland's faith, which inspired her to act on her calling rather than ignore it.

I

Julia, a patient of mine, was a wonderful and positive lady who was chronically tormented by her son's addiction to drugs and alcohol. This life-destroying situation had prevailed for years; Mark was in his mid-forties. I knew the only way to assist Julia was to help her change the way she dealt with her son; a real tough love was needed along with help from God.

In late 2012, Julia and her husband were scheduled to go on a cruise. She almost canceled the trip because she was so concerned about Mark's addiction. I encouraged her to go anyway, and in the end, she and her husband took my advice.

I had never met Mark, but I felt an inner calling to reach out to him; so I sent him a "Thinking of You" card. Not long afterwards he called me and we had a friendly conversation. Mark said he was on a good path at the time. He was off drugs and alcohol, had started music lessons, was exercising routinely, and had bought himself a new wardrobe.

Unfortunately, the "good path" was short lived. Mark soon became involved with a woman he had loved for years, a woman who had broken his heart various times in the past. When she rejected him yet again, he down-spiraled in the usual fashion of missing work (a family business), neglecting his hygiene, and traumatizing his family.

In May 2013, Mark's older brother, Ken, age forty-nine, died suddenly from an unsuspected brain aneurysm. The family was grief stricken, and Mark down-spiraled even further. Eventually, he came to me for help. Our doctor-patient journey began.

The best way for me to describe the next ten months of my non-judgmental care and support was that it was a time of prayer and faith. I prayed for Mark every day, feeling that I was holding space for God to do His miraculous work.

I felt encouraged when Mark came to all his appointments. In a fairly short time, he started sharing his feelings about things, situations, and people. What he didn't talk about, however, was his drug and alcohol use. I knew. I saw his blood pressure elevated without any other good explanation and watched his body language in the room.

Eventually, he admitted to *some* use. That admission at least enabled us to be on the same page. He knew he was pushing the limits. I knew he was pushing the limits.

A new girlfriend made her way into Mark's life around the time of his brother's death. She was a heroin addict and an unfit mother of a young son, who was eventually taken away from her. I would gently question Mark as to why she was in his life, since he had confessed his lack of attraction to her. He came to admit that he was very weak in spirit and needed her care, support, and friendship. They used drugs together.

In January 2014, Julia made the decision to fire Mark from their family business. Mark knew he had to get clean to get his job back, but he refused to go to rehab because he didn't believe in the twelve-step program. "What higher power?" he would say.

I had been praying for Mark and also for the words to talk with him about God and spirituality. After all, I felt it had been a distinct calling that got me involved in Mark's life. I figured that sooner or later we would engage in a discussion about God and prayer. However, he never brought it up and neither did I.

At one visit, though, he alluded to the fact that he felt comfortable in my care. He couldn't understand why I was kind and caring, since I knew the whole truth of his situation. He couldn't understand why I wasn't judging or rebuking him.

"Don't a lot of Christians go around pointing fingers at others?" he asked.

Needless to say, when he told me of his distaste for the twelve-step rehab program, I didn't challenge him except to ask about his plan to detoxify off the drugs. He and his new girlfriend were planning to do this together. Lo and behold, that process went much smoother than I thought! Then, however, came the challenge to stop drinking alcohol.

That undertaking was much more difficult. He had been drinking so much that he was vomiting twenty or more times a day and having just as many black and watery bowel movements daily. I strongly advised hospitalization. He refused, but did agree to see me for an appointment. I had to negotiate with him to get an upper endoscopy, and I started him on some medications to help with the symptoms. I ordered blood work, which was no longer normal. With very high liver enzymes, Mark knew he had to stop the alcohol. Therefore, I gave him a medication to prevent seizures from alcohol withdrawal. It was all misery for Mark, but he got through it.

On a Thursday morning in the middle of March, I awoke with a very bad feeling about Mark. I knew he had an appointment with me at 11:30 that day. It didn't feel like he was using drugs or alcohol again, but I knew *something* wasn't right. Was he beginning to weaken in his resolve to stay off drugs and alcohol? I came to the office and told my office manager about my feelings. She just figured he was reusing drugs or drinking again, but I still didn't believe that.

Mark missed his appointment with me for the first time. He called the following week to apologize profusely. My office manager reassured him that I was not angry with him, only concerned. He rescheduled his appointment for two and a half weeks later. My deep sadness and worry about Mark stayed with me.

On a Friday evening about five days before Mark's appointment, I was leaving an enjoyable outing with friends when I suddenly experienced a heavy, emotionally exhausted feeling. On the drive home, a severe, lancing head pain started from behind my left ear to the back of my head. I have never been one to get headaches. The pain baffled me.

As soon as I got home, I went to bed then proceeded to have a horrible night. I would sleep and then wake up from the pain, which seemed to worsen until the middle of the night. Finally the pain eased, and I was able to sleep.

In the morning, I received word from one of my colleagues that Mark had died during the night. I called his mom, Julia, right away and learned that at about 3:30 a.m. Friday, Mark had somehow fallen against a very sharp, exposed corner of a closet in the spare bedroom of his apartment and got a very long and deep head laceration. He didn't go to the hospital until about eight o'clock that morning. After the hospital sutured and stapled the head wound and determined that his vitals were okay, they released him. Mark returned to the apartment and slept off and on throughout the day. His girlfriend reported that he vomited some, then eventually stopped breathing.

When I called my office manager with the news, she informed me that Mark had called in around eleven o'clock Friday morning when he got back from the hospital. He left a persistent message. When she returned his call, Mark wanted her to let me know how much he appreciated and valued my care and time. He also wanted me to know he realized how much his parents loved and cared for him. He said he knew they had to fire him from the job in order for him to get clean. I think he knew it was the end.

I struggled and prayed about all of this that whole weekend, needing to get an answer from God. It came by Sunday evening. After talking to two very spiritually attuned friends, and after putting together all I knew, the picture became clear to me.

God had answered my prayer for Mark, just not in the way I had anticipated. Mark's death was an act of God's love, grace, and mercy. I *know* He brought Mark into heaven to be with his brother, Ken. There would be no more anxiety and insomnia. Mark would no longer be tormented by the feelings of wanting drugs and alcohol. He would finally experience unbelievable love, peace, and forgiveness. Unsavory people would no longer take advantage of Mark's kindness and weakness of spirit.

I felt so honored and privileged to have been part of Mark's last year of life and his salvation. Given all the people he knew in his life, including friends and family, Mark chose on his last day to call and reach out to my office. I knew deep in my heart it was to let me know that God saved him.

A couple weeks after his funeral, Julia stopped by my office to give me a gift that Mark had bought for me right before all of this happened. In cleaning out his apartment, she came across it and made sure to give it to me. She didn't understand the significance. I did.

It was a beautiful plant with a rock in the soil that said *Faith*. I was thrilled. This was the affirmation I needed. In dying, Mark was saved.

II

AS A PHYSICIAN, I was trained to save lives, so the idea of saving a death was new to me. I had been seeing a patient, Sally, for many years and had a cordial and respectful relationship with her. Over time it became apparent to me that Sally and her daughter Judy did not have a close relationship. In the last couple years, Judy began to accompany her mom to all our office visits because of Sally's declining health. It was through those visits that this ambivalent, and sometimes antagonistic, relationship between mother and daughter revealed itself to me. Having no background or details, I took their relationship at face value with no judgments.

In the last year, as Sally's health was noticeably diminishing, she was frequently admitted to the hospital. No longer able to live on her own, she would end up at skilled nursing facilities for some "rehab" between hospital stays. With her multiple serious medical conditions, it was unlikely that her health would improve significantly.

At our last office visit, both Sally's daughters, Judy and Colleen, accompanied her. That was the first time I had met Colleen. From that visit, some things became apparent to me. First, these sisters had a fairly good relationship with each other and both showed concern and care about their mother. Second, it became clear to me that Sally was prideful and stubbornly resistant to her daughters' feelings for her. I got the impression that Sally had spent her life not taking responsibility or accountability for her own hurtful actions and words or their negative effects on others. By the time of this visit, the daughters had found a personal care home for their mother, but Sally was bitter about the whole thing. I agreed with the daughters' decision to move her to that home.

Within a couple weeks of that visit, Sally was giving up, refusing to get out of bed, refusing to walk, and refusing to eat. I received a call from Judy asking if she should admit Sally to the hospital again. After a full discussion about Sally's state of health and mind, we entered into a realistic discussion about getting hospice on board. The next day, we enrolled her into hospice care at the personal care home.

The following morning as I was driving to work, I had an overwhelming sense that I should visit Sally and also that I should pray with her and for her. Yikes! I had never prayed out loud with any patient. I felt anxiety kicking in; yet, I had come to clearly know God's calling and knew He would give me the power and strength to do whatever needed to be done.

After seeing my last patient, I drove to the personal care home. Sally was lying in bed, happy to see me. Within two minutes, it became clear that she was distraught about not being forgiven by God for her mistakes in life.

"Have you been praying about it?" I asked.

"Yes," she answered weakly, "but I don't think He was listening, or maybe not answering."

I asked if she wanted to pray more, or if she wanted me to pray for her. She turned and looked me straight in the eyes.

"I need you to pray with me," she said.

I knew it. I knew this was coming. So, I held her hand, closed my eyes, bowed my head and prayed. I really don't even remember what came out of my mouth, but as I prayed, I felt incredible heat radiating out from my chest and upper abdominal area. It was quite a remarkable happening!

I knew there was more to do, for I heard that inner voice from my heart telling me that much healing still needed to take place for Sally's family. I had spoken with Judy and understood the hurt that her mother had inflicted for so many years. Sally apparently had always found something negative about everyone and tore people down. I could tell that Sally had not lived a happy life and had not been close to anyone, including her husband, who had died years earlier. So, for a couple of months, I made weekly trips to see her after work on Wednesdays.

My heart knew that Sally did feel love for the people in her life but she was too stubborn and proud to express it, or even to apologize when she hurt one of them. And so, with gentle but persistent suggestion and encouragement, I persuaded Sally to allow me to be her scribe. We wrote letters to her family members. I was able to help Sally make positive and loving statements that she simply was not able to vocalize herself. I knew what questions to ask: *What do you think is really great about her? What do you admire about him? What are you most proud of? What do you wish for her?* Then I put those answers into her letters.

It took several weeks to write the letters. On my last Wednesday visit, we finished the last of them. When I left, I hugged Sally "goodbye" as I always did, and told her I wouldn't be in the following week, for I would be on vacation. I drove away feeling that my job was perhaps done. On my way home, I stopped at the post office and mailed the last of the letters. In the end, her three children, two sisters, and two adult grandchildren received them.

When I returned from vacation, Sally's chart was on my desk. A sympathy card lay on the chart. She had passed away during the previous week.

I felt a sense of serenity, knowing she died feeling that God had forgiven her. I hoped those letters, her memorialized positive and loving words to her family, brought some healing to them. What an honor it had been to help her and her family experience her passing in more peace than they had known as a family.

Janine Rihmland, mother of a daughter and son, both college students, is the founder and head of The Health Center for Integrative Medicine located in Washington, Pennsylvania.

Right on Track

Kristin Avery

First of all I am not religious but absolutely spiritual. I have a deep connection to spirit, believe in angels and also that God is a beautiful Source Energy existing in all things. Although I've never had a near-death experience that I know of, I feel like I have many of the feelings and after effects that many NDE'rs have.

All my life I have felt very connected and drawn to old train tracks. I'm not sure what it is but I get this feeling of excitement and dèjá vu when I come across them. I often wonder if I had a connection from another life. I have always had that feeling.

The last several years I have lived in a town that is full of old weathered tracks that are no longer in use. They wind throughout this whole beautiful, nature-filled area. I love to take long walks on them, always going back in time thinking of who rode on those very tracks, where they went, and what life was like back then. I look down the tracks and wish I could hop on an old slow-moving train and go wherever it takes me.

For the last three years, every time I walk on them I look for a loosened spike to place on my bookshelf or mantle. I like the rustic look of an old railroad spike, and it also represents my love of the rails. I've spent countless hours enjoying walks on the tracks, and have never found a loose one.

Then one day as I was walking my two dogs on the tracks, I got this *knowing* that I WAS going to find one today! I smiled to myself and felt joyful inside. In fact I even stopped looking for one because I KNEW it would find ME. I even remember thinking, *I bet angels can stop time, place a spike for me to find, and start time again without my even knowing!* I laughed as I happily skipped from board to board.

I came to a bridge that went over a small creek. The smaller of my two dogs was frightened of walking over the slats because they were open and water was underneath, so I picked her up and carried her across. When I got to the other side I bent over to set her down, and there, right there, down through the last open slat of the track on the bridge, sitting by itself on a little part of the wood that held the bridge up, was a spike! Just lying there. It wasn't anywhere it even should have been and I had to have bent down right in THAT spot to see it, too. I reached my hand through and grasped it, *KNOWING* it was put there for me. My joyful, connected feeling stayed with me for days!

Things like this happen to me all the time and I take them as a sign of spirit, angels, and my mom saying "we are here, we see you, you are doing a great job." My spike is proudly displayed on my mantle with other special items as reminders that I am spiritually connected to the Source Energy that exists in all things.

Kristin Avery is a "50 years young" free spirit. The youngest of five siblings by five years, she learned to find solace in doing her own thing, which instilled in her a strong independence, strength, and sense of adventure. Her parents divorced when she was 13, causing her to spiral into depression, little self-love and years of rebellious floundering. At twenty-seven, she joined the USAF and became a nurse. For many years Kristin explored life as a single woman, learning from life's challenges such as both her parents dying when she was in her late 20s, a cancer diagnosis, and almost dying herself in the hospital due to sepsis. Feeling a spiritual connection, she looked into religion but found it too confining. Slowly she deepened her inner journey, and healed her own life by looking inward, reading books, taking courses, listening to meditations, and enjoying different teachers and speakers. She says she is amazed at how one great book or idea always leads to another of life's mystical interludes, signs, and synchronicities! She is now happily married and enjoys bike riding, kayaking, hiking, her pets, and continuing her personal inner journey.

His Name Shall Be Isaiah

Ed and Tiffany Craft

ED

SOME MIGHT SAY that Tiffany was my love at first sight. I saw her photo on a friend's Facebook page and asked for an introduction. Soon I "friended" her, then we were talking on the phone. She was living in Georgia and I was attending medical school in West Virginia. It didn't take us any time at all to fall crazy in love. Soon, Tiffany moved back to Pittsburgh where her parents live, about an hour from where my family lived. We started dating and were married a year later.

Unfortunately, our marriage got off to a rocky start. I had just started my surgery residency, working eighty hours a week with little time to spend with my loving new wife. Tiffany, a home health therapist, found herself alone during most of her leisure time. When we were at home together, I was usually tired, irritable and sometimes nasty. Rather than building a life together, we drifted apart.

Hoping to salvage our relationship, I changed the course of my career to family medicine. We moved to a town near Cleveland, Ohio where I was able to practice. Trying everything we could to save our marriage, Tiffany and I went to couples' counseling and also individual counseling, but I think our expiration date for marriage had passed us by.

Everything came to a head on a Friday in October 2012. I had plans to fly to San Diego the following morning to attend a conference. That afternoon during counseling, Tiffany told me she wanted a divorce and was leaving me. Her parents were coming from Pittsburgh to help her move back home. She added that she had reserved a room for me near the airport and announced that I would be receiving divorce papers in the mail. Feeling numb, I went home, packed my bags, and left for the airport hotel.

On my way from our apartment to the hotel, I called my mother to tell her about our separation. For some odd reason, I started to cry, not tears of unhappiness, but tears of joy! I should mention here that I grew up the son of a United Methodist minister in the West Virginia Conference. He had always taught me that when life gets rough, run to Jesus. In my confusion, I must have thought about that because the next thing I knew, I heard God plainly in my mind say, *Ed, I did this to you. I took Tiffany from you.*

Dumbfounded while driving, I asked, *What do you mean? You did this to me?*

He answered, *I have some things for you to do. You have not been listening. I had to take your wife away to spend time with you and get you back on track. I am giving you a promise of restoration.*

Okay, I replied, feeling that that I had experienced a genuine *calling* from Jesus.

By the time I returned from California, I was filled with grief and misery for losing Tiffany. The only person I told about our separation was my boss. I devoted all my time outside work to personal counseling, and also on deepening my relationship with God. My awareness began to bloom. My understanding of things I did to cause Tiffany's unhappiness grew within me. I could see that I had been selfish and mean. I also realized that anger and bitterness, which had been with me from childhood had spilled over to corrupt our loving relationship. Consequently, my life took an amazing turn!

During the following months I began having prophetic visions, dreams, and words for people. I was able to see things, know things, and say things which came to pass and also bene-fitted the recipients. I believe that this was God's way of showing me the fruits of His work. My faith was mightily strengthened.

Meanwhile, I had received a few sets of divorce papers from Tiffany, which I could not sign. By not signing, I believed I was keeping the door open for her return. Likewise, I wore my wedding band, did not see other women, and did not tell friends and acquaintances that Tiffany had left. I would call her number from time to time, but she rarely answered. If she did pick up, it was only to remind me to sign the papers and send them back. Regardless, I loved her and hoped she would come back.

One night as I sat reading the Bible, I asked God to change Tiffany's heart. He asked if I *really* believed that He could do that.

I answered, *Yes, I do.*

His answer was, *Sign her papers.*

What? I thought I hadn't heard correctly.

The answer came. Sign her papers.

I said, *Okay, Lord, I'm going to need a little bit of a promise. You gave me your promise of restoration back in October when Tiffany left me. It's now December. I need a little promise, here.*

He spoke: *From your wife's womb your first child will be a boy. You will name him Isaiah, which means "salvation of God."*

Okay, I replied. *That's good enough for me!* I kind of thought it odd that He said "from your wife's womb" because I was thinking, *where else do babies come from?* It seemed like an unusual thing to add.

The next day, I signed the divorce papers. Then I waited for a court summons.

In February, as Valentine's Day approached, the summons still had not arrived. Two months had gone by since I signed the papers. I couldn't understand what was happening. Tiffany had made it quite clear that she wanted a divorce, but she hadn't done anything with the papers. I took a chance and called to see if I could take her out for Valentine's Day. She refused and shouted that she still wanted a divorce.

On a Sunday morning a few weeks later while I was praying, I had a message from God. I was told to call my wife and deliver a message from Him to her. I don't recall the specific words of the message, but I do know that it wasn't one of warm fuzzies. It was a tough message, which I thought would make her angrier. After the last phone call, I was quite reluctant to call her. My head began to ache. By about nine-thirty that night, I gave in. After about ten rings, when I thought Tiffany wasn't picking up, she answered. At that point, we hadn't really talked except for her screaming at me to sign the divorce papers.

For some reason, this call was different. We actually *talked* to each other— for about an hour and a half! Then we switched to FaceTime! This was the first time I saw her since she left. I had called because the Lord had given me a message for her, which I expected to incite her fury. Realizing that we were actually looking at each other and *communicating,* (and that this was not of *my* doing) I told her I had something from God for her.

She said, "Okay."

I gave her the words that God had given me the day before, expecting her to be mad as a hornet. But she said, "No, I really felt that God was telling me that last week as well." To my surprise, she accepted it.

At that point I envisioned a golden hand enter her chest and pull out her heart. Immediately, her demeanor changed. Her scowl turned into a smile. The tone of her voice softened. She wanted to see me in person!

That was on Sunday. I drove to Pittsburgh on Tuesday after work. Shortly after we were together, Tiffany looked at me and said "I love you."

I hadn't heard those words from her for over six months! I had watched her spiritual transformation occur because she allowed it to. If she had not received and not allowed God to change her heart, nothing would have happened. The change was immediate and evident. We were joyfully reconciled.

We started dating again. Tiffany put her wedding ring back on and told me she had not turned in the papers because when she received them, she wasn't sure she wanted the divorce. That's when I experienced an aha moment! I thought of my reluctant ignorance when God had told me to sign the papers and also to call Tiffany with his message. My heart overflowed with gratitude.

TIFFANY

THE FIRST YEAR OF MARRIAGE is challenging for most couples. Ours was handicapped from the beginning. The day after we got back from our honeymoon, Ed started his first day of surgery residency. It was terrible. He was working all the time. I had moved from Pittsburgh to West Virginia, where I didn't know anybody. I felt isolated and lonely. My husband was always tired because he was working eighty hours a week. His tiredness made him mean and cranky. He would come home from work, and I would want to go out and do things. We would end up fighting. When it became clear that something had to give, Ed decided to go into family practice. We moved to Ohio, a little closer to Pittsburgh.

I expected the move to fix everything. Soon I realized that the destructive patterns established during our first year of marriage came with us. We went to counseling, but, for me, it was too late. I believe my mind had been made up even before we started counseling. There were some benefits, though. Ed became aware of some anger issues, and he worked on them. Even so, in my mind, change was impossible. I felt that to continue trying was just prolonging the inevitable. Wanting to get on with my life, I made the decision to leave Ed.

I moved back to Pittsburgh with my parents and drew up divorce papers. Ed and I didn't own a house or have children, so the procedure was uncomplicated. I sent him the papers, but he wouldn't sign them at first. We talked periodically about his signing the papers. That was the only communication we had, and those conversations were brief and angry. Then one day the papers came in the mail to my parents' house. I had already moved into my own apartment, but had not given Ed my address. I remember sitting at my mother's kitchen table, opening the envelope and looking at the signed papers. I realized at that moment that I wasn't sure if divorce was what I really wanted. I thought, *now I have the signed papers, but I don't know what I want to do with them.* Mom and Grandma were in the room with me.

I looked at Grandma and said, "Grandma, I'm not sure of what to do with these papers, now."

She said, "I thought you wanted a divorce."

"Yeah, I thought I did, too, but now that I have these signed papers, I don't know if that's what I want."

What I did know was that I was unhappy with the way I had been living and carrying on with my life. I had been dating different men, partying and drinking. I was only interested in doing my own thing. Even though I wasn't enamored with any of my dates, I never considered going back to Ed. I talked quite openly about my broken marriage and my reasons for leaving my husband.

I had left in October of 2012, and the papers arrived in early January of 2013. As I said, our only conversations were about his signing the papers. Every now and then Ed would call to talk to me, but I would hang up or simply not answer the phone.

One evening in February, the phone rang and I saw that it was Ed. I was home alone and just relaxing. At first I wasn't going to answer, but I knew he was probably curious about the divorce papers. I was also wondering about my own reticence about the papers, so I picked up. Surprisingly, we began having a normal conversation. We talked for over an hour. Then we switched to FaceTime and continued talking.

The whole time we talked, I knew in the back of my mind that *I needed to get my act together.* There I was, looking at Ed on Facetime and he was saying that I needed to get my life on track and get my act together. Normally I would have been angry when he said something like that to me, but I *knew* he was spot on. Also, other people close to me had said the same thing. I thought of the many times friends and acquaintances told me that I was making a mistake to divorce Ed. I remember one particular time I was getting my brakes fixed at the shop of a mechanic who was a friend of my parents. He knew what was going on with me, and he asked about how I was doing. A guy in the room looked at me and said "God doesn't want you to divorce your husband. You should stay with him." I thought to myself, *Who are you to tell me what I should do? Go fly a kite! I'm not staying with Ed!* So here's Ed saying to me what I had been hearing from others.

Then he said, "God wants you to straighten up your life and do what's right in your heart."

In that moment, something within me changed! I *knew* he was right. I think it was something deep down that I knew all along. It was probably the reason I didn't do anything with the signed divorce papers. My love for Ed, which I had suppressed, rose up within my heart. I think those words were what I needed to hear in that exact moment.

Ed came to see me in a few days and we began dating. I knew that I still loved him, and I put my wedding ring back on my finger. That was in February. The lease on my apartment wasn't up until June, so throughout those months, Ed would come to Pittsburgh or I would go to North Ridgeville, Ohio. We talked on the phone a lot. Our continued separation was helpful to restoring our loving relationship. It gave us time to heal and renew our trust in each other.

We began our lives together again and grew more loving and more joyful with each passing month. Deciding that we were ready to become parents, we planned to have a child. But conceiving a baby was not as easy as we thought. Many months went by, and pregnancy eluded us. Eventually we both underwent tests in a fertility clinic. The conclusion was "unexplained infertility." Over a period of a few years, we persevered through two cycles of artificial insemination using Ed's sperm. That didn't work either. We started consultations for in vitro fertilization. Ed was reluctant. He reminded me of God's promise that we would get pregnant and have a son. It was a struggle for us. In our happiness, we both longed to become loving parents.

After almost five years, we considered adoption. Ed and I chose an agency in Ohio, where we attended classes for prospective parents. Two home studies were required for adopting parents. We went through the first home study successfully and scheduled the second.

Shortly before the second home study was to take place, it became apparent that my breasts were enlarging. Ed suggested that I take a pregnancy test. I did, and it came out positive. *This cannot be right,* I thought. I called Ed upstairs and showed him the positive test.

"This has to be a false positive!" I exclaimed.

Ed said, "Get your jacket, we're going to the hospital."

"Why are we going to the hospital?" I asked.

"Because you're getting a blood test. A blood test will confirm whether or not you are pregnant."

The test was positive.

Nine months later, I gave birth to our precious son.

His name is Isaiah.

Edward Craft is a Family Practice Physician who lives with his wife, Tiffany, on the West side of Cleveland, OH. He is the author of *Restoring God's Marriage – Understanding God's Perspective on Us.* Tiffany was previously a Home Health Physical Therapist before deciding to stay home and raise little Isaiah. Both Ed and Tiffany have been very involved in their church, leading children's ministry in impoverished areas of Cleveland. They strive to follow God's direction in all areas of their lives.

Be Still

Craig Stephan

Editor's Note: This edited excerpt from the author's memoir, *Riding on Empty*, begins with Craig in Pittsburgh talking on the phone with his sister, Kris, in Ocala, Florida, prior to his trip there. Kris is telling him about their mother, a victim of cancer nearing the end of her life.

Kris said, "She seemed okay yesterday, but today she almost collapsed on me. We stopped to eat and when we were walking into the restaurant her knees buckled! I caught her on the way down. She didn't even have the strength to walk from the car to the restaurant. I need to get her a wheelchair. I'm going to call Hospice tomorrow to set things up."

"I'll leave Monday morning. Will you please tell Mom I should be there by Tuesday afternoon?"

"Sure, honey! All Mom's talked about for the past two days is your visit."

My emotions became more than I could handle. It took everything I had to finish, "I'll talk to you tomorrow."

I sat in silence with the door to my office closed. *How was I going to deal with this?* I was angry, frustrated, and sad. No, not sad. I was flat-out, low-down miserable. All of my emotions, which had been building up for months, were coming to the surface at once.

Without warning a deluge of tears uncontrollably poured down my face. My soul was broken. I was tired of being tired.

Where was the answer I was looking for to save me? *Please God, give me the strength to see me through this!*

Leaning back in my chair, I stared at the wall right above my desk. Where would my strength come from? *Where should I turn?*

Just then, a black silhouette appeared on the surface of the wall. It was Jesus, as plain as day.

I should have been stunned, but I wasn't. In fact, the exact opposite occurred. I felt as though I was being lifted into a new dimension. My body felt relaxed, warm, and comforted. My self-defeating thoughts were replaced with complete optimism. I felt instantly transformed into a new body of faith. My concerns and anguish vanished. For the first time, I felt absolutely, unequivocally certain Mom was in good hands.

* * *

On Monday morning, I packed my truck and quickly left for Ocala. I was on a mission from God. He was going to help me get through this. My faith was at an all-time high. I couldn't wait to tell Mom what had happened.

It was 1:00 when I pulled in, and sure enough, Mom was waiting on the front porch. *God, I love her!* I hopped out of the truck and jumped up on the front porch. She slowly lifted herself from her chair. We beamed at each another and I gently hugged her. She looked great!

"Kris is inside preparing lunch for us. Let's go in. After that long drive you must be hungry!"

"Well, I had a little breakfast but I can always eat Kris's food."

My sister was in the kitchen preparing what smelled like one of her gourmet dishes. She came from around the counter to give me a hug then Kris set the table with her European flair. I helped Mom take her seat as we prepared to feast.

"If I may," I said, "I want to share something with you that happened to me the other night."

I made eye contact with them to indicate my seriousness. I had their full attention.

"Kris, after I got off the phone with you the other night, my concerns came to a head. I really had a down moment and started to panic. I sat back in my office chair and, just then, on the wall above my desk appeared an outline of Jesus." Speechless, they looked at me in amazement. I seized the opportunity to continue. "I can't really describe the feelings that came over me. In fact, it's almost impossible to describe in words what I felt. What's most important is that I feel obligated to share with the two of you the message I received."

They sat quietly and let me continue.

"Mom, I can promise that you are in His hands. He assured me that He is completely in control of your future." I looked from Mom to Kris to see their reaction.

"Craig," Mom exclaimed joyfully, as she grasped my hand, "what a gift you've brought us!" Her eyes welled with tears as she continued, deeply moved by my experience, "And I am so grateful that happened to you, too." Her pale blue eyes bored into mine.

"May I ask you a question?" she added.

"Of course," I replied, squeezing her hand reassuringly.

"You told Kris that right before you had your vision and received your message, you were feeling particularly down. Can you remember anything else about what you were thinking? For example, do you remember asking God for help?"

"Let's see, I was feeling lost, thinking about everyone in my life and wondering who I could turn to for help."

"Yes, that sounds like how it happened to me, too! You were asking for help when you received your vision. Remember that."

"What happened to you, Mom?" Kris asked.

"Here's what happened. I was going through a hard spell, I couldn't see my way clear. It was like I'd gone into the woods, and pulled the covers over my head.

It was Wednesday, March 26, 1986, and though it was a beautiful afternoon when I should have been outside enjoying the sun, I went to bed.

I had been in a blur and hardly cognizant of my surroundings. My knees had been so weak, it was all I could do to stand, Not only this, but I was overwhelmed with my own worthlessness, so that I could see nothing else in this world. Truly, I had been searching my anguish, I called out, *'God, help!'* And that is all I could say.

The most extraordinary thing happened.

Immediately, I was quieted, stilled, at peace and, furthermore, all the hurt, the real hurt and emotional pain that had been consuming me, real physical pain throughout my body, and especially in my chest, was *gone.*

I have never known such peace in all my life. It was warm and wonderful, and I felt as though I had been scooped up and was being held! I couldn't move. I tried, but couldn't. Now, on occasion, I have been in a bad state and crying and sobbing and then decided to stop, but it always took me a few minutes to quiet myself down. This was not like that at all.

I was not quiet, I was *quieted.* And when after several minutes I tried to move again, a voice... an inner voice...said, 'Be still, and know that I am God!' Of course, this is one of my favorite passages from scripture, and one cannot prove that it was not my inner speaker, but I am convinced it was the God within me, at least. Then, several minutes went by, and I said, calmly, 'What do I do?' and the voice said, 'Nothing. Be still and know that I am God.'

After a long time of this stillness and peace, these words came to me, 'As with a little child, I will take you by the hand and lead you out of the desert.' Now, this is not one of the Bible verses I have ever thought about. I have never thought about my state of being as analogous to being in a desert!

"I wish you had told me all of this back then, Mom," Kris said reaching out to hold her other hand. "Please, tell us, what happened next."

Mom continued.

> The voice said "Give it up," and for the first time in my life I was able to give up some things I wasn't hereto even aware of, not the least of which is my pathological need to give my love and also my need of acceptance from those I love. There were also other things, my ego and my desires, for instance. I lay there in the same position for fifteen or twenty minutes and then I was able to get up for the first time in weeks. My knees did not shake, my mind was clear, my spirits raised, The rest of that day, and after, I felt alive, interested, filled with serenity. I knew then what happened: I was forgiven. Though I had sought the Lord's forgiveness all my life, this was the first time I had known forgiveness. I felt as though I had truly been reborn and that my past was all behind me.

Articulating each word and speaking very slowly, she firmly stressed, "Believe me, this was not of my doing, for I had been trying to forget and maybe even forgive, but could not." She took a deep breath, shaking her head deliberately from side to side. "If nothing else, the physical change, the strength that I had that day and after that happened attested to it." She finished speaking, and with a satisfied look, leaned back in her chair.

"Mom," Kris said, "thank you. That means a lot to me. I had always wondered what happened to you when you returned home.

"You mean, you were feeling so depressed then, and yet you'd listen to me when I called in distress about my love life?" I asked in amazement at her selflessness and my own self-centered insensitivity.

"Craig," she replied, "give it up!" She continued to speak in a gentle manner, "You know when I decided to stop the experimental treatment at MD Anderson, I never really explained myself to you children."

"You didn't have to, Mom," I told her.

"I didn't want to tell you about it because I didn't want you to think I was flipped out. But now you know. It was such a life-changing experience, which to this day will see me to the end.

"I hadn't thought about this in years, but one of the things I let go of that day was my financial insecurity of not being able to complete my degree. You remember how hard your father worked and how guilty I felt asking him to pay for my tuition? Well, one of the things I was feeling anxious about was how I was going to pay for the next term. A few days after my spiritual experience, I learned I had won the full scholarship. Craig," Mom added, "do you remember the time you came to visit us and we went to the seashore in Galveston?"

"Of course, I do."

"I brought home a wonderful souvenir of that day. Kris, honey, go get that little poster on my night table, okay?"

Kris returned momentarily with a framed white poster, which stated in bold black print, "Be still and know that I am God. Psalm 46:10."

Craig Stephan is the author of *Riding on Empty,* an inspiring memoir about his life-long struggle with dyslexia and his close relationship with his devoted mother who lovingly nurtured his growth into manhood and realized dreams.

Into the Blue

Canela Michelle Meyers

When I write those words, Near Death Experience, I do wonder a bit—is what happened a NDE? I feel it to be so from the effect it had on me. Who can really know unless there were doctors present who could say that I was officially dead... which there were not until after the NDE already happened.

In approximately 2003, I was a chaperone for a school outing to the ice skating rink. Both my sons were participating that day. When everybody arrived, parents and teachers made sure that the children had helmets on. It never occurred to me to wear one. I don't remember if other parents or teachers did wear them or not. I hadn't ever worn one while skating.

It was the first time I had skated since I was a teenager. At first I was very wobbly, then gradually, my skating legs came back. Music was playing and I was having more and more fun as my confidence grew.

I went skating past my sons and said "Hey you guys, watch me—I can skate backwards!" I turned backwards, laughing, skating backwards in time to the music, and having a ball. Then the back edge of one of the skates caught on the ice. I fell hard on my tailbone then smacked the base of my skull on the ice.

When my head hit the ice, I seemed to continue floating down, down, down as though I were under the ice, into a vast light-blue light. I was no longer in a body. I was marveling at the freedom, the expansiveness, the utter delight of floating as light! There was nothing at all that located "me" anywhere.

"I" wasn't anything that showed up as something. At the same time, I could see and feel in all directions, this open, light blue space—it was light, free, expansive, a blessing, loving, and went on forever, there was no edge to it. There was nothing tethering me to anything, no lines of connection, nothing at all except this open, free, beautiful, so beautiful, light blue light that I was/am.

Then above me I saw people up on the ice, very far away... so far, they looked like small ants. It was like I was two-football-fields below them. I knew they were people but I felt no connection to them. I felt completely neutral towards them, even though those people included my sons. I felt no connection to them at all...they were just an image up there that seemed to have nothing to do with what I was as this blue light.

Then I heard, or I thought, or I am not sure how it was because it wasn't in "words": *"That will not work without This."* Somehow that registered. I heard it. In that instant, I was back in my body looking up at everyone, attempting to remember how to work the body, feeling my arms, and relearning how to lift them.

I was taken to the hospital, where a doctor checked me out. He listened to what I had experienced and said it sounded like I was consciously unconscious. He just shrugged his shoulders and insisted that I have someone with me for the next forty-eight hours because of my condition.

Even though I had a huge goose-egg bump on my head, a concussion, and a very sore tailbone, I felt I had been given an incredible gift. A gift that I understood and received immediately, and that also expanded over time in many directions.

One of the main ways that this experience supported me was that I looked at things differently. During the two years preceding my fall on the ice, five of my aunts and uncles had let go of their bodies—they had died.

Because of this experience, instead of feeling sad, I felt happy for them! If there was a chance that they went into the blue light when they died, then that was a very wonderful thing to happen! I missed being with them in person, but I felt happy to even imagine them in the floating blue light.

I had faced death myself in many ways prior to this happening. This NDE, though, was quite different from those other ways of meeting death. Being in the blue light, I felt like I was being shown that mortal death is perhaps, not such a "bad" happening. Not that I want people to die or that I don't care—I do care. I am human and prefer people to live, especially those people close to me. However, this experience changed me in how I feel about mortal death. It opened up this possibility (because of my own direct experience) that letting go of the body might be beautiful when it happens.

I have no wish to die, which, in some moments, I do find rather strange because even remembering that vast blue expansive light gives me a peaceful feeling…I wonder that I do not desire it. And yet there is no desire for it. It is just here with me, in that it was experienced as it was, as a support to myself and to others when I share how this happened. People can feel the light as I talk about it, and this has often soothed others who are grieving the death of someone close to them.

Canela Michelle Meyers is a Satsang Facilitator, a Kundalini Yoga Instructor, a Reiki Master and author of *Right Here, Right Now Meditations* (www.canelamichelle.com). You can watch her interviews on *Buddha at the Gas Pump* and *Conscious TV*.

Somewhere in Time

Anonymous

Traveling back in time to my childhood home in South Florida wouldn't reveal any overt signs of a religious or spiritual life. I was a typical kid born into a quasi-Lutheran/Catholic household yet was never encouraged to attend church, other than at Christmas and Easter. Though I didn't have the vocabulary to describe it, I was highly empathic, sensing the feelings of others, including animals, as if they were my very self on a deeper level. This became an access portal to the spiritual dimension. On one occasion, after watching a cicada insect that appeared to be suffering while it was dying, I harbored a sense of anguish for days.

Still, nothing else from those early years stands out more than a vivid dream I once had when I was about six years old. Within the dream I was walking on a path toward a mountain that I know now to be Arunachala, a sacred hill in Tiruvannammalai, India. The most significant memory I have from the dream is that I was taking slow steps alongside a man wearing what appeared to me as a diaper. While strolling along, I stumbled and he caught me, pulling me back onto the path. I later came to realize that the man was the already deceased Indian sage by the name of Sri Ramana Maharshi.

To that point my entire life, as far as I can remember, had been like a pleasant movie. My youth was fairly typical for a middle class child. Yet, one day, after being encouraged by my parents to defend myself against a much larger boy who was pushing me around, I beat him bloody, and from then on began getting into violent fights and trouble quite often. I didn't care much for academics but did fairly well in school. I preferred physical activities and enjoyed playing sports, where I achieved national recognition and success. But deep within, I was seeking something more, something with meaning.

When I was about fifteen, I was drawn to the movie *Somewhere in Time* starring Christopher Reeve and Jane Seymour. I watched it over and over again. The story is about a young playwright, Richard Collier, who is approached by an elderly lady who comes to a college play he has written and directed. Approaching him in a crowd, amongst his peers, she hands him a gold pocket watch and says, "Come back to me," before turning and mysteriously disappearing into the crowd. Intrigued, he keeps the watch. A few years later, after becoming a professional playwright, Richard feels the need to escape from the stress of writing his recently commissioned play and ends up at the Grand Hotel located on Mackinac Island, Michigan. There, while he is browsing the hotel's hall of history, he is mystically drawn to a vintage photograph of a beautiful young actress, Elise MeKenna from the early 1900s. Compelled to learn all he can about her, he discovers that not only was she the old woman who had given him the gold watch at his college play, but she had died that very night. Desperate to find her, the playwright finds that the woman had read a book on self-hypnosis, which he then teaches himself, allowing him to travel back in time and find her. When he does, she does not know who he is, so he courts her and these soul mates fall in love…again!? However, fate takes a turn and as they plan their future together, Richard's hypnosis is disrupted and he is whisked back through time to the present, where he dies of a broken heart. The last scene of the film shows Elise MeKenna in a misty beyond reaching out her hand. As Richard walks slowly toward her, she takes his hand and they unite.

This movie was important to me because it was a metaphor for finding *the* love, *the* woman and soul mate. I watched this movie at least twenty times, showing it to every girl I liked.

Though I was rather promiscuous in my youth, I really wasn't interested in being with many different girls but yearned to find *the* one. In fact, many times it seemed like I was actually looking for someone in particular.

After high school graduation, I received a scholarship to a top university, where I became a successful football player. I was a regular guy except for the fact that I was an introvert, so when my friends were out at bars and frat houses partying, I was content to stay in and listen to love ballads, entertaining fantasies of a faceless girl I hoped to meet one day.

Under the suggestion of my coach, I enrolled in a sport psychology class where I fell in love with meditation and creative visualization, a more primitive version of what is now commonly called the Law of Attraction.

After college I played professional football briefly until a knee injury ended my career. One week later, I learned that my mother had been diagnosed with terminal cancer. As a young man whose dreams of playing pro ball were pretty much shattered, it felt as though I had come to a critical point in my life. During the one-week window between the football injury and returning home, I was invited to go to Mackinac Island with my girlfriend and her family. Thrilled for the opportunity to visit the place where my favorite movie had been filmed, of course I went.

One morning we took a walk around the entire island, which was about eight miles. I remember enjoying the beauty and appreciating the absence of noisy cars, which were not allowed on the island. To my delight, only bicycles, horses and buggies were permitted. Eventually we came to a cemetery and someone suggested we play a game of searching to locate the oldest tombstone. As I moved to step between two of the stones, I smacked my shin on the corner of one. Kneeling down to grab my shin, I saw it—my exact birth date carved on the gravestone inches from my face. In shock, my mind stopped! A jolt of energy pierced through my entire body and I felt a strange expansion I had not felt before. I had a profound recollection and revelation, where it seemed my mind was trying to piece things together.

My attraction to this particular island was one thing, but its relevance was specifically associated with a story about a man who returned to a past time to find a woman. And here I was on Mackinac Island near the Grand Hotel staring at a tombstone inscribed with a past date that matched my birth date!

Looking back, I can certainly say that was a pivotal moment. Until that instant, I had accepted the traditional views of social and religious institutions, government, and all that I had been taught, never questioning their veracity. Until then I didn't really want to think about anything except girls and sports, and in that order. Yet here I was, for the first time, considering the possibility of reincarnation. The idea was completely foreign to me. But to my surprise, I was overcome with the certainty... it was true.

A couple of weeks later, I found myself watching the movie *The Reincarnation of Peter Proud* without knowing why. In the past I would have changed the channel looking for sports or action movies, but I didn't. A paradigm had shattered. Because I began considering, if reincarnation were possible and I had been wrong about it all this time, then what else had I been wrong about? How many other things could I be mistaken about?

Once that train of thought began, I couldn't stop it. I began questioning everyone and everything. I wondered if all I had ever learned was a lie. I stopped going to church and stopped believing that I had to be "saved" or that anybody was going to "save" me. That marked the beginning of my spiritual quest.

My life took many turns during subsequent years and I practiced meditation until I was meditating for hours daily: just sitting in the stillness. Not long after, I was involved personally with two jnanis (Self-realized teachers), traveled to India several times, and experienced what is known in Zen as a satori: absorption in the bliss of oneness. Soon, I gave away all my possessions except some clothes and books before moving to an ashram that disseminated the teachings of Sri Ramana Maharshi. Although he passed in 1950, he was essentially known throughout spiritual circles as the master of masters. When I arrived, I saw his picture and recognized him as the man who caught me and helped me back onto the path in my vivid childhood dream. In a later vision, Sri Ramana Maharshi and I were standing in a house together when he turned to me and communicated that I had a calling. Then he placed a seed in my hand, which symbolized that I was to pass on the teachings of Self-inquiry. I turned and handed the seed to a woman who was to my left. With this vision, though I did not know who she was, I knew instantly that she was the woman I had been looking for all my life.

Years later, while serving as a spiritual teacher in 2004, I met her. As she sat down upon entering class, I had a flash of the woman in my vision, and though she did not look the same, I knew she was the woman to whom I handed the seed. Two weeks later we were married.

Ironically she, like Richard Collier from the movie, had come to seek relief from the stress of a career related to writing. The evening when she and I first watched the movie *Somewhere in Time* together, I realized that night that this was not only the woman from my dream with Sri Ramana, but also the woman I had been looking for my whole life. I knew I had been with her before; it was like coming home. One other peculiar synchronicity was that precisely when Christopher Reeve's *Somewhere in Time* character, Richard Collier, died in the movie, the actual person Christopher Reeve died as we watched the end of the movie. We cried tears of deep affection when we woke up to the news report the following morning.

Though the synchronicities in this life have been many, the most significant, however had its roots in my vision of Sri Ramana Maharshi. I have since followed his instruction that I teach Self-inquiry, and along with my wife have helped spread the fruits from that seed throughout the world.

Editor's Note: This author preferred not to use his name. I verify the authenticity of this story.

Angelic Messengers in the Stillness of Night

Virgi Bohn Peters

I slipped into bed exhausted from another day at the hospital and endless hours of waiting for another precious fifteen-minute visit with my husband in the Intensive Care Unit, and more conversations with his nurses and doctors, and keeping family and friends up-to-date on John's condition. You'd think I could quickly doze off, but the memory of two nights previous kept popping into my head. I had been urgently called back to the hospital when John's condition suddenly turned grave.

When I arrived the staff was doing everything they could to keep him alive, but his purplish skin tones were revealing otherwise. I stood by helplessly wondering *Is this it? Will John die?* His doctors were hoping to do a CT Scan before surgery, but a moment later they were forced to forget that idea and rush him straight into the operating room. Their life-saving efforts worked. Afterwards, John was on a ventilator and extremely weak. But he was alive!

Eventually I was able to unwind from my fears by focusing on my breathing and just trust, trust that John was in good hands—God's hands. This allowed my mind and body to sink into much needed rest until I drifted off into sleep.

Then suddenly I was awakened in what seemed like the wee hours of the morn. I felt I was in a place beyond time in what seemed like an amphitheater of angelic beings. Their radiance was brilliant and their love phenomenal. To my surprise, John was in their midst. I heard no sounds, I just felt many angelic beings lavishing their heavenly love on John, which I was somehow receiving and witnessing as well.

The angels were holding him within their loving presence, reassuring him that everything was well, and that John had a choice to make: *Do you want to return to your earthly existence or remain in the heavenly realm?* John's soul-sensual response was: *I want to go back to earth.*

A moment thereafter I was back in a normal time continuum, lying in the darkness, alone in my bed. Although I was comfortable and warm I was feeling disoriented and wondering *What did I just experience? Was it a dream or was it a celestial encounter, and what did it mean?*

In the last couple weeks John had been through so much: two back-to-back surgeries and his ongoing issues with radiation fibrosis from his cancer treatment. Images of John struggling to breathe the other night surfaced again, and then suddenly the reality of what happened became clear to me. This time he didn't almost die. *This time he did die, and he made a choice to return!*

As this revelation was clarifying in my mind I felt profound compassion for John and all he had gone through being a cancer patient. As I lay in bed, I reviewed the history of his illness. Many couldn't believe he was still alive much less an eleven-year survivor of non small-cell lung cancer, which has a survival rate of three percent. When John was diagnosed in 1989, he had two lobes of his right lung surgically removed and as much radiation as a body could handle. He refused chemotherapy as he reasoned that if he didn't have long to live, he didn't want to spend time going through nauseating sickness.

With a three-percent chance of survival, John started searching his mind for any hope of what he might do, and remembered hearing about people being cured of cancer with alternative therapies. He started to think outside the box of allopathic medicine, but didn't have any idea how to get information about alternative therapies. So, he prayed for guidance and a little while later he found a group in Butler County that had regular monthly meetings about alternative therapies. There was no Internet in those days, but this volunteer-based group provided the contact information so John could do his own research. He got information on several alternative therapies that showed promise before finding the Gerson Therapy (www.gerson.org). He learned that this was a proven nutritional therapy for cancer and other degenerative diseases. He thought and prayed about it a lot, as this program would necessitate a radical change in his diet and lifestyle. John finally decided that he would do it—if he really needed to.

By the ninth month after his cancer surgery and radiation treatments, John was feeling like a windup toy that was winding down. Then a video bronchoscope revealed the cancer was back. John's "if he really needed to" moment was at hand. The doctors said they would have to surgically remove what was left of his right lung, and that he couldn't refuse chemotherapy this time. As long as I live, I will never forget his answer! It was courageous and brave.

He said, "Not only am I refusing the chemotherapy, I am refusing the surgery."

The doctors were surprised. One doctor hit the table with his fist and emphatically told John that he was committing suicide.

John replied, "I may die, but it won't be at your hands, so it's neither your concern nor decision to make. I am my own CEO!"

For fifteen months John was on the full protocol of the Gerson therapy to cleanse his body. After just three weeks, he experienced an increase in his energy and had a sense of *knowing* the therapy was working. He *knew* the cancerous condition would disappear. And it did!

Feeling awe-inspired from remembering John's courageous braveness, I got out of bed to call the hospital, but not to check to see if John was okay. I wanted to let the staff know John was going to live! I asked them to give him a clipboard with paper and pencil so he could communicate, since he was still on a ventilator. The nurse's reaction to my assuredness was one of surprise and curiosity, "How can you be so sure?" she inquired. "He's very weak and we almost lost him."

"I know," I replied. "And I also know in my heart and soul he's not ready to die! He's got more living to do on earth."

John lived another decade, becoming a 21-year survivor of lung cancer before passing away—not from cancer, for he was still cancer free, but from the side effects of cancer treatment. That decade was well spent. He shared his experience with other cancer patients seeking answers, and we traveled in our RV, went square dancing several times a week, and enjoyed our lives together.

Being a human on earth is a very precious gift, and we can only experience it while we breathe. May we learn to allow each *breath of life* to be for us a mystical interlude between the terrestrial world of forms and the celestial realms of heaven and discover the joy that sets us free.

Virgi Bohn Peters, retired from the business world, now works and plays at staying mentally, emotionally, physically and spiritually healthy. She loves square and round dancing, yoga, walking, meditating, creating colorful, nutritionally dense meals, reading, and researching. She also writes about the universal wisdom inherent in the profound spiritual movement founded by Jesus Christ, which has within its practices the power to change the way we see the world.

Dreams

Pat DeBee

It's said that everybody dreams. I've talked to friends who say they rarely remember their dreams. I'm happy to say that I do remember a lot of mine, and I've come to realize that some dreams are very special. They are the ones that not only don't leave my memory, but also remain fresh as though they just occurred. Three of those dreams, which happened during three consecutive nights, were quite extraordinary for three reasons: they were about the same subject, they were in the same setting, and each was a continuation of the preceding dream.

I was an only child of thirteen living with my parents in a three-story house in Pittsburgh. The house was too large for a family of three, so my parents rented the second floor to various couples to supplement our income. It was in that house, a few days after Christmas, that these dreams about my mother occurred.

Dad had brought home a newly cut pine tree, and the three of us adorned it with cherished ornaments, bubble lights and tinsel, as was our Christmas tradition. On Christmas morning we unwrapped our gifts and later enjoyed our Christmas turkey dinner. That Christmas, like many before, was low key with no unusual stress or health issues.

On the third night after Christmas, the first dream occurred. My mother and I were in a glass booth on opposite sides of a transparent partition. We could see and hear each other, but could not touch. My mother stood expressionless. With no emotion, she spoke as though stating a fact, "Patty, I'm going to die." I started crying and shouting, "No, Mother, no! No, No!" She was unresponsive. This was most unusual. As an only child, I was accustomed to getting my way after crying and pleading.

The second dream occurred the next night. We were back in the glass booth, but this time when I looked at my mother on the opposite side of the glass partition, I knew she was dead. As in the previous night's dream, she was in a standing position, but I knew her spirit had left her body.

On the fifth night after Christmas, my dream placed me back inside the glass booth, but my mother was not on the other side. Instead, I watched her funeral and burial take place in the distance beyond the transparent partition.

The next night was New Year's Eve. My parents had a couple over to play canasta and enjoy some pop and snacks. When it was time for me to go to bed, I protested. "Mommy, I don't want to go to sleep! I keep having bad dreams that something bad is going to happen to you!" But, she consoled me with, "Don't worry, honey. It's okay. Nothing's going to happen." She kissed me goodnight and sent me off to bed.

When I awoke the next morning, our big house was strangely quiet. Discovering that neither of my parents was home, I went upstairs and asked our tenant where they were. She told me that my mom had suffered a stroke during the night and my dad was with her at West Penn Hospital.

I later learned that in the middle of the night, Mom woke up with "the worst headache of her life" and told dad to call 911. Assuming that the call was from another New Year's Eve drunk, the paramedics took longer than usual to arrive. Our little cocker spaniel, Cindy, who usually barked at strangers, did not make a sound as people came in and out of the house, and Mother was wheeled to the ambulance. I heard nothing, did not dream, and slept peacefully.

My mom did not die from her stroke that night. She lived for twelve more years, suffering from partial paralysis on her left side, and even surviving breast cancer. Tragically, a little more than two years from that night, my father was suddenly killed in a fall when scaffolding collapsed on his job as a painter. These dreadful, catastrophic events terminated my childhood and catapulted me into an early adulthood.

I quickly learned how to not only take care of myself, but also how to become a caregiver for Mom. We helped each other as best we could throughout her surviving years. Sometimes she seemed to snap out of her confusion and try to "go on" for my sake. I am deeply grateful that she was able to see me graduate from college and get married. I am also thankful for every millisecond that Mom and I shared.

Although my mother did not die as portrayed in my series of dreams, I had lost my mother. I no longer had the mom who took my friend and me on the trolley to movies, the annual Kennywood picnic, clothes shopping, and dentist and doctor checkups. I had lost the mom who helped me study for spelling bees, memorize historical dates, recite poetry, and practice adding up lengthy columns of figures. Worst of all, I had lost the mom who cared for my every need including setting my hair in bobby pins, laundering my clothes, cooking, cleaning, shopping, and helping me in all that I attempted.

On New Year's Day, a door slammed shut on my childhood. I awoke to a new family constellation, one that required early maturity from me and much support from my teachers, church friends, neighbors, and classmates. My life had changed forever.

Although I have never had a series of consecutive dreams like those again, I have many times pondered their prophetic message. In retrospect, I feel that my mother's spirit was attempting to communicate that the upcoming changes were neither her choice nor mine, but were inevitable. I sense now that she was trying to help me accept the unacceptable.

I will always appreciate the uniqueness of those very special dreams as further proof of our mother-daughter bond of love and also the awe that such a "mystical interlude" inspires.

Pat DeBee is a retired language teacher and mother of a daughter and son. She resides near Pittsburgh, Pennsylvania, with her husband and continues to explore her dreams and intuitive abilities. I have come to know Pat as a loving, caring, and compassionate human being.

My Life-Saving Accident

Tim Powers

My mother was hospitalized in critical condition. I arrived at the facility at about seven on the morning of June 28, 2016. Her doctor ushered me into a private room and told me that Mom was near death. She advised me to summon our family.

After my sister arrived, I made a call to my friend who is a funeral director. I told him that Mom was dying, and I didn't think I would be able to make the arrangements after she passed. My sister and I made the necessary decisions for a funeral. Afterward I went to my tattoo shop, disconnected all the machinery, including the water cooler, and posted a note on the door that that read, "Due to family emergency, we will be closed until further notice." Even as I was doing those things, I wondered why I felt compelled to do them, considering the fact that Mom was still alive.

Mother's condition remained critical for days. On July 4th, she was delirious. On July 5th, she made an incredible rebound! After a few days of constant monitoring, the doctor said we should make arrangements for home care. We set those wheels in motion, but I was still wary about Mom's recovery since the doctor had given her a matter of hours to live less than a week earlier. The tentative date for her discharge was July 16th.

Sunday, July 10th was a perfect summer day, which inspired my wife, Daeneen, and me to ride our motorcycle to the hospital. I had been spending every day with Mom, having not returned to work since the day I closed. After we arrived, I ran a few errands for things Mom wanted. Later, Daeneen and I decided to accept a friend's invitation for a visit to his farm. It offered a change of routine and a scenic motorcycle ride through the country.

We were greeted with warm hospitality and enjoyed the afternoon in the environment of the spacious farm. As we were leaving we agreed that the day was indeed ideal for traveling on a motorcycle. Our ride home through the country was delightful until we topped a hill that made a slight turn to the left. Rounding the bend, I saw a deer jump off the hillside.

I shouted, "Deer!" and hit the brake.

Daeneen lurched forward, screaming, "What?"

Hooves hit the pavement! We struck the deer! The bike hit the ground.

I found myself on the ground about three feet from a doe's face, gazing into her large dark eyes. I distinctly remember thinking, *I'm sorry*. I swear, in the deer's eyes, I saw *I'm sorry* come right back at me.

Crash bars saved us from being crushed, yet the force of the impact cracked my helmet. Daeneen got off the bike and asked if I was all right. I kept demanding to know from her that she was unhurt. The doe scrambled to its feet and ran off. I struggled to my feet gasping for breath. Feeling intense pain, I rested on the hillside and asked Daeneen to call 911.

She shouted, "I can't get a signal here!"

"Walk up the road," I answered.

"I don't want to leave you," she said. After a pause she reluctantly began to walk.

Just then, a car came by and stopped. An older couple got out and asked if we needed help. Daeneen told them she couldn't get a signal to call for help. Fortunately, the couple lived in the next house a short distance away, and the wife went to make the call. Meanwhile, the gent had a sheet in his car and held it above me to block out the sun. I was gasping for breath and started to feel pain just about everywhere, but especially on my left side.

Eventually the ambulance arrived and we headed for a medical center about eleven miles away. Meanwhile the EMT, who told me to call him Matt, determined that both my lungs had collapsed. I heard him tell the driver that we needed to call for a "bird." My relentless phobia of heights caused me to protest with as much energy as I could muster. Matt explained that the care I needed was not available at the medical center. I had to be taken to UPMC Presbyterian Hospital, about forty miles away through Pittsburgh traffic.

"I won't get on a helicopter," I said, "just drive there." I closed my eyes.

Matt told the driver to head for Pittsburgh. A while later, he got my attention and said, "Mr. Powers, we're five miles from the hospital and we're stuck in gridlock traffic. We need to call for a helicopter."

"Matt, I told you once; I will not get on a helicopter," I said.

"Sir, I don't know if we can get you there in time," he replied with exasperation.

With full force, I said, "If you'd turn the siren on, everybody will get out of your way!"

Eyeing me quizzically he said, "Sir, we've had the siren on since we picked you up on Kelly Road."

To this day, I don't remember ever hearing that siren. It seems I remember everything that happened on the way to the hospital, but I've blocked out the sound of the siren.

I closed my eyes again, and the next thing I knew, they were taking me out of the ambulance on a stretcher. People came from everywhere and started asking the EMT and me questions upon questions. I was wheeled into the hospital and taken straight into a room with a CT scanner. Just as the scan was started, everything stopped. I found myself rushed out of that room and down a very cold hallway. A man with a mask over his face said to me, "You've been bleeding internally. You're filling up with blood. We are going to the OR now!"

Three days later, I awoke in a hospital room.

My wife started to cry when she saw that I was conscious.

Once I realized where I was, I said, "I've been in this room before." She thought I was talking that way because of the drugs.

A nurse came in. I recognized her and said, "Hey. How've you been?"

She said, "I'm sorry. Do you know me?"

"I don't remember your name, but I remember you."

She looked puzzled. "You remember me from what?"

"From the last time I was here," I said.

She glanced at my wife and asked, "What were you in here for before, sir?"

I answered, "Same exact injuries." I realized I didn't know what my injuries were. The nurse finished up, and left.

A little later, I don't recall whether my wife was there or not, another nurse came into the room. I looked at her and said, "I remember you, too."

"You do?" she asked.

"Yes," I said. "I was here before with the same injuries, and you and the other girl took care of me."

She shook her head and said, "Sir, I don't think you were ever here before." She finished what she was doing and left.

Then, a man walked in wearing an odd expression. That's when I thought the nurses must be talking about me at the nurse's desk. He said, "I'll bet you don't remember me."

"I don't remember your name," I said, "but I believe you're the doctor who pulled me out of the CT thing and took me into surgery."

He looked stunned. "Do you seriously remember that?" he asked.

"I certainly do," I said.

"I'm Dr. Neal," he said. "You're absolutely right. I took you out of the machine and rushed you to surgery." He continued, "You had a ruptured spleen, which we removed. You also had many broken ribs on your left side, collapsed lungs, and a broken left clavicle. After losing two and a half pints of blood, you were almost running on empty."

A female doctor had slipped into the room while Dr. Neal talked. When he finished, he turned to her.

"Mr. Powers," she said, "I'm about to tell you something you're not going to fully comprehend or understand. This accident actually saved your life."

"What are you talking about?" I asked.

"When we opened you up, your organs were badly damaged and discolored. We kept the incision open and put you on life support in order to assess the damage. After removing your spleen, we excised a severely injured part of your pancreas and sent it to pathology. The report came back showing pancreatic cancer."

My expression must have been one of shock and alarm, for she placed her hand on my arm and said, "Oh, sir, it's all right. You're going to be fine. The cancer had just started to grow. We removed it, one hundred percent! We went back and removed a safe margin, then followed up with many biopsies. I can guarantee that your pancreas is now clear of cancer."

Still confused, I asked if I should get an oncologist. She reassured me that I had nothing to worry about. They had removed all the diseased tissue.

At that point, my head was reeling.

After they left, another young nurse came into the room. I looked at her and said, "I remember you, too!"

With a bit of attitude she said, "Mr. Powers, I don't think you remember me at all. You were never here before."

"Oh yes, I certainly was!" I answered.

"So, when would that have been?" she asked with skepticism.

"Well, I really can't remember when," I said.

"Right," she said. "Sir, I can tell you that you were never in this hospital before."

"I'm sorry," I said reluctantly, "but I'd swear you were the nurse who gave me the tetnus shot."

Her face froze. "Mr. Powers," she said, "I'm here to give you a tetnus shot right now."

I looked her square in the eye and said, "I know you are, because we've done this before."

"I don't know about that," she responded, "but I'm here now to do it."

I said, "I know you are, because we've done this before."

She gave me the shot and left.

A short time passed and a tall, blonde nurse entered. I looked at her face, but did not get that familiar feeling I had been getting with the other people. I said a weak, "Hello."

She stepped forward and said, "I know you! You're Tim from Magic Ink Tattoo."

Suddenly, the table had turned. "How do you know that?" I asked.

"Because you did my first tattoo fourteen years ago. My name's Jamie," she answered.

I did not remember her face. I asked if she liked the tattoo.

"This is weird," she said. "I've had you on my mind. I was going to call you and set up an appointment to get another tattoo. And here you are!"

When she was gone, I wondered why the only person I hadn't recognized that day was a nurse I had met earlier in life. I tried to wrap my head around all the strange and shocking occurrences of the day.

Another astonishing surprise came the following day. One of the nurses came in to repack the incision. I was lying with my head on a pillow as she removed my hospital gown and pulled back the sheet. I noticed her eyes grow wide.

She said, "Mr. Powers, what was your accident again?"

"A deer jumped off a hillside and I hit it with my Harley," I said.

"What side was the deer on?" she asked.

"It was on my left," I answered.

"Just like your legs!"

"Excuse me?" I asked.

"Just like your legs!"

"I don't know what you're talking about," I answered, confused.

"Really?" she asked, while she pushed the button to raise the top of the bed until I could see my legs. They were straight and resting together side by side.

"Oh my God!" I gulped.

When I was teaching myself to tattoo, I practiced my craft by tattooing on myself. On my right upper thigh I had tattooed a Harley heading toward my left leg. My left thigh showed a deer leaping over a log and heading toward the motorcycle on the opposite thigh!

"How long ago did you do these tattoos?" asked the nurse.

"About twenty-seven years ago," I said, realizing that I had looked past those tattoos for years, failing to even notice them.

"You know what you should do when you get home? Tattoo some lottery numbers on your body!" she laughed.

For days afterward, nurses and hospital personnel, from receptionists to janitors, streamed into my room to look at the tattoos on my thighs.

During my thirty-six days in the trauma unit, I had time to wonder about the strange way I *knew* the hospital room and the doctors and nurses. I also had a vision in my head of what I looked like lying on the operating table. *I* was *me*, looking down from above at *me* lying on a table with an open incision. I told my wife I felt I had been prepared for the accident. I still carry that vision.

Months later after I was back to work and getting back to a normal life, I returned to Presbyterian Hospital to thank the staff for their great care. Jamie, the girl who had received my tattoo, saw me walking down the hall, and she started to cry.

"Why, Jamie?" I asked. "All my injuries were internal. Nothing was wrong with my legs. I could have walked even then."

"No, Tim," she explained. "When you left here, we didn't think you'd make it."

"Well, why was I discharged, then?"

"It was because insurance said you were no longer considered a *trauma* patient. We had no choice but to discharge you to rehab at the time."

I thought about my discharge and how I had requested a

rehab facility close to my home. The doctors said that wasn't an option, and sent me to North Hills Passavant Hospital instead. I followed up Jamie's revelation by questioning one of my doctors that day. He explained that my injuries were severe enough that if complications occurred during rehab, an ambulance might not have been able to transfer me to a hospital in time to save me. Sending me to a hospital facility as a rehab patient was for my own protection.

His report supported my belief that I had been prepared for the accident. Never once during the entire ordeal did I think I might die. I certainly had no fear of dying, even if I had been told that I was close to death. I just can't figure it out.

My wife tells me I talk at night when I seem to be dreaming. If someone were to ask me, I would tell them I don't dream. If I do, I certainly don't remember any dream I've ever had.

On the other hand, this entire episode, beginning with my mother's crisis, seems like one long, mystical dream.

Reviewing my whole experience with a clear mind, I feel I was guided and protected by Divine intervention.

It begins with the day I was distraught over what I thought was my mom's imminent death. That news prompted me to close my business and post a note on the door. That note remained there for a total of eight months until I returned to work after my accident.

When my wife was unable to get a signal to call for help after our accident, a couple, who coincidentally lived in the next house, appeared on the spot.

My pancreatic cancer would likely have remained undetected until I was beyond help if it hadn't been for the accident.

My *knowing* the hospital staff, along with my *vision* of seeing myself on the operating table, tell me that something mystical was going on.

The doctors' decision to send me to a rehab *hospital* was also a providential life saver. As it turned out, I had some critical complications during rehab. The doctors had made the right call.

And then there is the prophetic tattoo on my thighs.

In the end, I feel I can call this whole experience a Divine mystical interlude.

Tim Powers, after working many years as a Database Analyst for a national credit bureau, made a radical career change by opening Magic Ink Tattoo in Monaca, Pennsylvania, a business more fitting to his "people person" demeanor. A motorcycle enthusiast for more than thirty years, he and his wife, Daeneen, travel around the country in their motorhome toy hauler with their Harley Davidson. They enjoy motorcycle riding wherever they travel. It is no surprise that Tim's story involves his Harley bike.

Love from Beyond the Veil

Nancy Aloi

The first time it happened was in 2004. I was driving my Honda Accord on my way to work. The all-too familiar smell of Copenhagen smokeless tobacco permeated the cabin of my car. Instantly, I thought of my father who always had a pinch tucked in his lower lip. Dad passed in 1987, but seventeen years later, that smell was still distinctly and instantly recognizable. Doubt made me lower the windows, thinking maybe I was mistaking an engine odor. But the smell remained. I drove on with a smile, thinking of my father.

That was the first time, but not the last. Throughout that year and into 2005, the not-so-pleasant tobacco aroma assaulted my senses time and time again. It would come upon me at random times. In those days, I was a middle school principal. The smell would permeate my office as I sat at my desk. At first I assumed my assistant might have confiscated tobacco from a wayward student. I'd check my desk drawers. Nothing!

Another time, I sat in a meeting with my administrative colleagues. The smell of "chew" as my dad called it, hit me with force. It seemed I couldn't escape it.

I wasn't sure if the odor was simply coming from my memory. That acrid scent had been embedded in my olfactory from an early age. (As youngsters, my siblings and I were occasionally called upon to empty Dad's spittoon. We'd argue over whose turn it was, as none of us relished the task.) But finally, on one occasion, a colleague who was also a close friend did get a whiff. It made me feel giddy to have confirmation from another that I wasn't just imagining the odor.

Gradually, I began to accept that the aroma of Copenhagen was my father's way of announcing his presence. From then on, each time the scent returned, I silently acknowledged him with love. With a chuckle, I still wondered, though, why he chose such an unpleasant way of getting my attention.

In hindsight, I believe he was trying to warn me of an impending maelstrom about to turn my life upside down. In the summer of 2005, my *happy* marriage of twenty-nine years came to a devastating end. In the aftermath of humiliation and pending divorce, I found myself utterly alone. Shell-shocked and broken, it was also the first time in a long time that I'd slept alone. During that dark period of time, there was no smell of Copenhagen. But soon, I became aware of something else entering my space.

One night, shortly after my separation, I was startled awake by a feeling that someone was standing next to my bed, near my shoulder. With the room too dark for visibility, I sensed more than saw a small female presence. Oddly, I felt no fear. Within a few seconds, the feeling was gone. I told myself it must have been a dream, as the dogs hadn't even stirred from their corners of the room.

I felt my visitor arrive again a week or two later. This time, I silently acknowledged the presence and welcomed *her*. Once again, the feeling vanished within seconds. Over the next few months, the visits began to occur more often, and slowly began to be more pronounced.

I would be awakened from my sleep by a feeling that I could only describe as a cat pouncing onto the bed. The first time it occurred, I reached down to pet the cat I sometimes watched for my daughter, only to realize that the cat wasn't in the house that night.

The visits occurred again and again. Each time, the visitor announced herself with the light pounce, which gradually progressed into soft, cat-like steps around my body. The nocturnal visits continued for more than a year, even after

I moved to a new home. I always gave a silent welcome and acknowledgement to the gentle, comforting presence.

The ultimate visit was a dramatic one. Lying on my back with my arms across my chest, I was just drifting into a light sleep when I felt the familiar pounce. Instead of feeling the usual feline-like steps, I felt hands on both sides of my body, firmly tucking the covers around my form, just as my grandmother had always done when I was a child. The covers were pinned so tightly, I was unable to move my arms. For the first time since the visits began, I was frightened. Silently I told the presence she had gone too far. Instantly, the feeling vanished and my arms were freed. Sadly, that was the last time my visitor made herself known to me in that way.

A little over a year after my marriage ended, I went to visit a friend who had lost his wife to cancer the previous year. I pulled into his driveway, put the car into park, set the emergency brake, and was about to open the door when the delightful aroma of freshly baked bread filled the car, just as the Copenhagen smell began two years earlier.

The smell evoked the sweetest childhood memories. My dad was a cement contractor who worked seasonally. On frigid winter days, too cold for him to work outside, he stayed home and baked bread for our large Italian family. When my siblings and I arrived home from school for lunch, that heavenly aroma greeted us as we ran through the front door. The dining room table would be filled with dozens of loaves just out of the oven. My brothers, sisters, and I would get to swipe the tops of the loaves with butter while they were still hot. And then, while the bread was still steaming, Daddy would cut thick slices for our lunch. Nothing would ever taste better!

When my car filled with that sweet smell, I breathed in deeply, this time, *knowing* it was my father! I sat with his presence for a few minutes, feeling loved and comforted before approaching my friend's door.

During the visit, my long-time friend nervously revealed that his feelings for me were more romantic than friendly in nature. Weighing the gravity of his words, I made a hasty exit that evening; but within a short time, I found myself returning his feelings.

My dear friend and I eventually married and have been enjoying a delightful new life together with our large combined family. Looking back, it has become clear that through the sweet aroma of freshly baked bread on that fateful night, my father was reassuring me that love and happiness were returning to my life. And he did it in the sweetest of ways!

A few years ago, I visited an intuit who had the gift of communicating with those who had crossed the veil. My grandmother came through and announced that she had been my nighttime visitor when I was alone. She also conveyed that she was as startled as I had been that I could feel her tucking the blankets around me. And she was equally as surprised that she could actually feel me!

The visits from my father and grandmother from across the veil have been transformative. I no longer fear death. The experiences have reassured me that our spirits live on eternally and we are all still deeply connected by our abiding love.

I now know that our loved ones are with us always, trying to guide and comfort us, if we only recognize and accept their help.

Editor's Note: My close friend **Nancy Aloi** is a former educator who started her career teaching children with special needs and ended it as superintendent of a school district in the Pittsburgh suburbs. My friend has always kept the needs of students at the forefront of her career. She now enjoys retirement as wife, mother, and Nonna to her two grandsons, while continuing her life of loving service to the needs of extended family, friends, and neighbors. In addition Nancy volunteers her time and experience by serving on the boards of organizations providing education and human services. Her mystical interludes have been transformational in helping her realize the eternal nature of spirit.

Visiting Yesterday

Anonymous

My wife and I travel internationally often. We have enjoyed visits to Cambodia, France, Italy, Turkey, and Croatia for example. My usual reaction when I arrive in a new country and city is a combination of anxiousness, nervousness, and trepidation until I learn my way around the new area. Our visit to the city of Prague in the Czech Republic in 2011 was strikingly different. Not only did I not have any of those feelings, I felt right at home. I felt peaceful, calm, and completely relaxed!

Why I felt that way befuddled me at first. I had no ties whatsoever to that country. My father's family came from Scotland, and my mother's family came from France. But somehow I *knew* to take bus 19 to the end, then transfer to trolley car 26 to get to the central area of Prague. It was a feeling *I am home.*

When we reached the central gathering area of the city, everything felt familiar. As I watched the town hall clock operate, I *knew* that was one of many times I had done so. I had a deep sense that I had lived in Prague in a previous life.

When we returned to our home in southwest Pennsylvania, I had a nagging desire to explore the possibility of having lived in Prague in a former life. After researching the subject of past life regression, I found a "regression analyst" and made an appointment. It was shortly after our return from Prague that I was entering another new experience, this time with some anxiety, nervousness, and trepidation.

I was soon put at ease, and through careful guidance, I found myself back in Prague, standing in the central gathering area. I knew the year was 1749.

Looking down at my feet, I saw that I was wearing black knickers, knee-length white socks, and dark shoes topped with gold buckles. Additionally, I was in a woolen type green coat, and wore a dark triangular hat. I seemed to be in my early twenties standing alone amid a crowd of people. I could smell the smoke from various cooking fires, in the fall season. I sensed that the gathering was about some type of festival. I glanced over my right shoulder and noted an open field with light brown tall grass. (I recognized that field as the same location where a small church now stands. My wife and I visited the church during our trip.) I then looked straight before me and could see a portion of the St. Charles Bridge, which is a tourist's *must-see* today. The analyst then gradually returned me to my present day, ending the session.

Later I researched the church located in the space where I saw the open field. It was built in the year 1761, twelve years after my past life vision. I have no doubt that I lived a prior life in Prague Czechoslovakia in the year 1749. To this day, when I see or read anything about Prague, I return mentally to the peace and calm I experienced being there.

As a result of this experience, I now believe that people experience past lives. I also ponder my Christian beliefs about death and the afterlife, which do not embrace the concept of reincarnation.

Editor's Note: This author preferred not to use his name. I verify the authenticity of this story.

Dr. Antonio

Jody Nowry

In February of 2006 my sister Celeste and I flew to the Palace Resort at Riviera Maya in Mexico for a free vacation. It was free because a year earlier Celeste's vacation at the Palace Resort had been interrupted by a hurricane. Both of us teachers, we scheduled our trip over President's Day weekend to minimize our use of personal days. The resort was all-inclusive, so all we had to do was buy tickets and board a plane. I would be turning fifty while there. What could be better than taking a break from my job and wintry weather to celebrate my fiftieth birthday in sunny Riviera Maya? Not much!

We arrived on Thursday and checked into our exquisite room. The newly refurbished resort was all that we could hope for: several inviting pools, full spa, juice bars, four and five-star restaurants, and the shimmering Gulf of Mexico! Feeling blessed, we did nothing for the first two days but relax in our luxurious surroundings. We sunbathed in the afternoons and dined on elegantly served gourmet meals in the evenings.

After dinner on Saturday night, we decided to explore a part of the resort we hadn't yet visited. The area was almost refurbished but some construction was still going on. Unlike construction sites in the USA, this construction area had no flash fencing or caution tape.

We strolled along the sidewalks and saw what looked like a gigantic porcelain urn projecting from the middle of a deep, narrow quadrangle, which appeared to be an empty pool. Our curiosity was piqued, so we walked closer to investigate. As we got nearer we could see that it was lit inside with a very high diving board as part of the structure. We later learned that the urn was a diving well for Acapulco diving performances.

Celeste moved to the opposite side while I remained where I stood. We chatted across the narrow empty pool. I walked on a few steps while commenting about something to my sister. She didn't respond. Silence prevailed. I realized I had just heard a thud! I broke into a run, calling her name. There was no outside lighting so I cautiously approached where I thought she should be. A slab of cement stopped my foot, and I looked down at cement steps leading to a dark hole. My sister's white jacket was visible at the bottom of the hole!

Screaming for help, I descended the steps while frantically reviewing CPR technique in my head. She was unmoving, but breathing. I shouted repeatedly, "Celeste, can you hear me." Security guards came and simply watched as I checked Celeste's vital signs.

Eventually, she responded. "What happened? My head hurts." I was relieved to hear what I thought that was a lucid response. I put my sister's arm around my shoulders and crawled up the steps with her. The guards made no move to help. When we reached the top, they helped us into their golf cart and said they'd take us to the building where our room was located. I objected and asked them to take us to the main building where the infirmary was located.

When we arrived in the main hall, patrons were dancing and dining. A scowling resort manager rushed over and angrily accused us of drunkenness. I sternly said, "Call a doctor. Now!"

He complied. Soon a doctor arrived. He assessed my sister's condition and called an ambulance. Leaving Celeste with the doctor, I ran back to our room for our identification and credit cards.

The ambulance was not equipped with a cervical collar or a backboard. Celeste was loaded onto a gurney, which was bungeed to the compartment's four corners. After I swiped my credit card to pay for the ambulance service, the paramedics allowed me to sit in front with them.

We rode for forty-five minutes to the Cancun Hospital while I listened to my sister careening about in back, literally bouncing off of the sides. As we pulled up to the hospital, I hoped and prayed that she would receive proper care there. MISTAKE! Our expectations of receiving medical care commensurate with that in the United States were dashed. This hospital was basically just a storefront in a very bad part of town.

The hospital administrator met me at the ambulance, demanding to know who would be paying for the patient. No How is your sister? or What happened to her? but rather, Who's paying? and How?

Scared and frazzled, I screamed, "I have money! Take care of my sister!"

Not to happen! Not until I swiped a credit card again. Then she was taken from the ambulance and admitted.

Celeste was very disoriented and agitated by this time. I later learned through doctors and research that she was exhibiting affects of a traumatic brain injury (TBI). When she failed to cooperate, they threatened to put her in jail! I asked to have her put into a medically induced coma before she hurt herself even more. Their response was that they did not have enough medicine to do that—even though she was the only patient in the hospital.

While my sister was taken into an exam area, I was forced to sit in a waiting room with four security guards who were watching pornography on the TV. They wouldn't allow me to go back and see Celeste. I asked to use a phone. In 2006 there was no signal in that part of Mexico for our cell phones. Knowing that, Celeste and I had brought phone cards to pay for calls home. The guards said I would have to use the pay phone outside, but I shouldn't go out there because the drug dealers and prostitutes owned the street at night. So I waited, prayed and snuck back to see my sister as often as I could.

At daybreak, I went to the pay phone. It was broken! Desperate, I jammed a pencil into the receiver. By some miracle, the phone came to life! I called my husband and asked him to give Celeste's daughter, Beth, the waiting room phone number.

A female doctor was on call that morning. She seemed competent and somewhat compassionate. She called a neurosurgeon when Celeste did not respond to their limited treatment. He came, did a few X-rays (akin to 1960 dental X-rays) and decided she would have to be transported to Tomography, another facility for a CT scan. My hope was revived as I thought we were going to a REAL hospital where Celeste would get decent care.

We got back into the ambulance, another credit card swipe, and off we went. We drove to a back street with ramshackle buildings and pulled up to one with filthy windows and no sign of anything that would indicate that it was a medical facility. They unloaded my sister into the alley and proceeded to knock on the door. NO one was home at Tomography.

By now, brain fluid was leaking from my sister's ears; Siamese cats were circling her gurney in the hot sun. The paramedics pulled out their phones. Up to that point I had tried to remain cool, afraid that even minimal care would go away if I panicked. But in that moment, I lost all control and started shrieking, howling and raging at God and my dead mother!

I recall wailing, "Do something Maxine, this is your child!"

As I paced, praying and pleading, a white Mercedes Benz, circa 1970's pulled up to the alley. An older gentleman in a white suit stepped out and introduced himself as Dr. Antonio. He asked me what was going on. Shaking, I blurted out my desperate circumstances.

Dr. Antonio immediately took out a cell phone, made a few calls, and almost instantly someone showed up to unlock the Tomography building. The hospital administrator also showed up!

Once inside, we were met by a technician who removed Celeste to radiology for the CT scan. Dr. Antonio went to the receptionist desk and gently asked, "What do you want to see done here?"

My response was immediate, "I want my sister out of Mexico by sunset this evening!"

Dr. Antonio chuckled and made a phone call. He spoke on

the phone for a few minutes, then handed it to me saying, "This is Thomas. He is in Texas. Speak with him and tell me if you trust him."

I took the phone and one of the kindest voices I have ever heard came over the line saying "Hi, Jody. My name is Thomas and I am going to do everything in my power to help your sister." This was the most positive thing I had heard in eighteen hours! I told Thomas what I knew. We both asked many questions.

He told me he worked for an agency that did air ambulance service and would try to get a crew together, but acknowledged that it was Sunday and a holiday weekend, so it could be tough. He was ninety percent sure that Celeste's health insurance would pay for most of it, but because it was Sunday, we couldn't contact her agency. He advised me to put together enough credit to pay the thirty-five thousand dollars just in case it would not be covered.

Meanwhile, I arranged with Celeste's daughter, Beth, the credit needed to cover the expense. Celeste's son located the necessary medical records to complete the transactions.

Much to my chagrin, I was told that we had to return to the hospital in Cancun. Dr. Antonio graciously came with us. We had to be careful not to let hospital personnel know of our plan because they wanted us to take their air ambulance out on Tuesday for ninety thousand dollars. Amazingly, Dr. Antonio and Thomas arranged a 5:00 p.m. departure from the Cancun airport.

I had to return to the resort hotel to pack our things and check out, but I was afraid to leave Celeste alone at the hospital. Dr. Antonio promised to stay with her, while a hotel shuttle was arranged to take me back to the hotel then deliver me to the airport. As I walked out the door with great trepidation, Thomas assured me by phone that Celeste would be safely transported to the airport by ambulance for the 5:00 p.m. flight. I was to meet her there.

When I got to the resort, the director, who the night before accused us of being drunk, was now, ever so solicitous.

"What can I do to help?" he asked kindly. I asked for a club sandwich and a bottle of water and hurried to our room.

In forty-five minutes I was packed, showered and ready to leave for the airport. I phoned Thomas for explicit instructions on where to enter the airport to avoid customs, a description of the plane, and its identifying numbers.

I got to the airport at about 4:45 p.m. Everything checked out as Thomas had instructed, but I had fifteen long minutes to wait until the air ambulance and my sister arrived. I don't think I breathed during that interim. When the plane came in and landed I cried with relief. The pilot and the paramedics came off the plane, surrounded me with their arms and we all prayed. But Celeste still wasn't there. Coming unglued, I called Thomas. He reached the hospital and we found out that my sister was enroute, but stuck in traffic.

The ambulance arrived twenty-five minutes later and we quickly boarded the plane. My sister was still very combative. Out of concern that she was doing irreparable damage to an already damaged brain, I asked the paramedics if they could sedate her. They discarded the Mexican bandages and gave her an injection. Then they made a bed for me. I was surprised by the kindness of the gesture. They said I needed to de-stress for my own well-being. My stress had been the last thing I thought about. I was only grateful that we were taking off as the sun was setting in Cancun that Sunday evening, just as I had asked of Dr. Antonio.

We had to fly low in the sky to prevent pressure from further damaging my sister's brain. The crew and medics were wonderfully competent. They kept me in good spirits with positive updates on Celeste and with stories of their rescues. Under normal circumstances I would not have been allowed to accompany my sister in the plane. Our six pieces of luggage would definitely have been banned. They couldn't have been more accommodating!

We landed at a private airport in San Antonio, Texas. I soon learned that for insurance to cover expenses, we had to go to the United States trauma unit closest to Cancun. I had hoped to get to Pittsburgh, but after our harrowing experience, any place in the US was fine by me.

We traveled by ambulance to Methodist Hospital, University of Texas, San Antonio. The staff was excellent and after many tests that night the doctor on call assured me that although my sister was very sick, her brain appeared to have stopped swelling in spite of the many bleeds. They had booked a room for me in the hotel across the street and an orderly was waiting to take me there. They insisted I go sleep.

My sister stayed in the Neuroscience Critical Care Unit at Methodist for a week, then the Critical Care Unit, before being transferred to a Health South Rehab in San Antonio for two more weeks. I had to return to work during this period, but Thomas visited my sister in the hospital. The nurses took my calls several times a day, and Celeste's children and I visited on the weekends.

Finally, we were able to drive Celeste home to another Health South Rehab in Sewickley, Pennsylvania for ten more days. Throughout this time, we were in constant contact with Thomas. We continue to communicate with him via email to this day.

My sister had a tough recovery. We are thankful that she did recover. All the doctors who have seen her since the accident have told her that she is a walking miracle. One physician said it best: "You do realize that you should be dead or at best another Christopher Reeves." Celeste's residual damage includes a lack of smell and taste along with a few vestibular problems. She has been able to return to her job as middle school choral director.

Wanting to thank Dr. Antonio, I emailed Thomas for his contact information. I was stunned to learn that Thomas didn't know whom I was talking about!

I said, "But Thomas, he called you from his phone like you were his best friend!"

Thomas was mystified. He said when the call came, he thought he was speaking to a hospital administrator.

I called the hospital in Cancun. They had no record of a Dr. Antonio!

Looking back, I recall that Dr. Antonio appeared when I was railing at my mother in that alley. He was in a white Mercedes and dressed in a white suit. Not only did he look like my dad, he bore my dad's name. In hindsight, we wonder if perhaps those coincidences were in place to enable me to immediately trust him.

Although we will never solve the mystery of Dr. Antonio, we do know for sure that he appeared in our moment of desperation to save Celeste from death or a lifetime of disabling paralysis and/or brain damage.

We are deeply grateful to our Guardian Angel or Dr. Antonio for seeing us through and granting us this miraculous mystical interlude.

Jody Nowry is a retired English teacher from the Central Valley School District north of Pittsburgh, Pennsylvania. She and her husband Ron have three children and six grandchildren. Jody loves volunteering at the local housing projects, exercising, reading and spending as much time as possible with her grandchildren.

Ladybugs and Hummingbirds

Nancy van Alphen

My mother passed away in 2001. She loved ladybugs and dolphins. Over the years, whenever I had the rare occasion to see a dolphin, I would think of her. Ladybugs were less rare. I came to associate them with my mother, especially when I visited her grave where a ladybug might crawl over my hand or sit on the gravestone seeming to watch me. I wanted to believe that somehow it was a sign from my mom, but ultimately I concluded it was just wishful thinking.

By the fall of 2017, I had experienced a series of spiritually transformative experiences, yet remained cautiously skeptical. I attended a major conference about near death studies. There I heard Nancy Rynes describe her remarkable near-death experience of visiting heaven and learning many things from her spirit guides. A woman asked if spirits took on animal forms to visit loved ones still on Earth. Nancy answered that it was more likely that spirits direct their energy to animals, sending them to a loved one at just the right place and time, often when that loved one asks for a sign. I thought of the ladybugs at my mother's grave. The fact that Nancy Rynes came from the same background of disbelief as I had, made me wonder if those ladybugs really were signs from my mother.

Not long after the conference, I sat on my back-deck hammock swing while taking a midday break from my home office. As I twirled gently in the swing, admiring the beauty of nature in my backyard, I found myself missing my mom. I realized that I hadn't seen any ladybugs since I moved from Ohio to New Jersey a couple of years earlier. *Perhaps they aren't common to the area,* I thought. *Something to look up later.*

I wanted to ask Mom to send me a ladybug as a sign, but I didn't want it to be impossible for her. At the conference, I heard some things I had read about, particularly that our souls reach different levels of growth over many lifetimes, and we continue to learn on the other side. I didn't know at what level my mom might be, so I picked something easier, and instead asked for a bird. Despite what mainstream society may think of my spiritual experiences and beliefs, I'm still a logical-thinking kind-a gal.

My backyard is a bird sanctuary with the most beautiful of bright red cardinals; blue jays nearly the size of squirrels; yellow and red finches; soft gray doves; chubby little chickadees; woodpeckers of several varieties; and a host of other birds swooping over the grass and through the woods less than twenty yards from my deck. They vie for sunflower seeds and mill worms from one of the backyard feeders and for space at the birdbath to groom in fresh rainwater. So asking for a bird made sense.

I talked to my mom for a bit, sharing simple things like how my life was going, and how my daughter, whom she'd taken care of when I was a young, divorced mother, was now graduating and excelling in her area of study. And I told her how I missed her. I wondered if she was able to hear me and whether she was happy. Remembering Nancy Ryne's talk, I knew belief was crucial to connecting with the spirit world. Fully believing my mom could and would respond, I asked her to send a bird directly to me. Then I sat in silence.

In a matter of just a few minutes, a shiny green hummingbird flew right up to me! It flitted at eye level only ten inches away, on the left side of my face. I followed it with my eyes only, not wanting to scare it with a turn of my head as it moved to the right side of my face and flitted there for several seconds again before moving directly in front of me. I was nose to beak with this delicate little bird, so close I could feel the wind from its wings beating up and down at Mach speed. My heart raced. Mom! I knew in my soul she'd heard me. Finally the little hummingbird soared out from under the covered porch and high into the treetops, the motor-like sound of its wings fading as it went.

I hadn't considered a hummingbird when asking my mother to send me a sign. I imagined that one of the many songbirds might land on the deck railing next to me, or even on my leg. Our hummingbird feeders are located toward the opposite end of the house, about twenty yards from my hammock swing. Though the hummers sometimes mingle among the flowers in my deck planters, they were never frequent visitors to that area.

But this would not be the only time I would encounter a hummingbird sent by my mother. A few weeks later I heard from my sister that she and her boyfriend broke up. It was tough on her because they loved each other, but their different lifestyles made a relationship impossible. I sat on my deck swing after the call and prayed for my sister and her boyfriend, asking that they both be given strength to move on and find happiness. Then I asked Mom, if possible, to be with my sister and bring her comfort. I didn't ask for a sign.

I went back inside for about fifteen minutes to take care of some chores, then stepped back out onto the deck, closing the sliding screen door with one hand and holding a glass of water with the other. I took two steps from the door when a hummingbird bolted at me from the right side, as if it had been lying in wait for me to finally come out of the house! I tensed my shoulders and froze as the hummingbird flitted again at eye level, circling my head, face forward in a jerky rotation, until we were again beak to nose for a few seconds before it soared off in the direction from which it had come. Without a doubt, I realized my mom was letting me know she'd heard my request.

Shortly after these experiences, I shared them with my good friend, Emily, and she asked me to write about them for this book. As I sat at my computer to begin writing, I thought about whether I should leave out the fact that I had always associated ladybugs with my mom. That wasn't really important to the experiences, after all. I received an answer when a hummingbird got my attention by banging into my office window. Looking up, I watched it make a beeline to my bright red patio umbrella, upon which I had hung a fan pull in the shape of a whimsical ladybug. The hummingbird hovered right next to the ladybug for an inordinate amount of time, at least by hummingbird standards. My estimate is ten to fifteen seconds. But it was enough for me to know exactly what it meant, and who'd arranged the symbolic meeting of the hummingbird and ladybug.

Nancy van Alphen is a work-from-home marketing analyst who has experienced several surprising, spiritually transformative events. These have altered her perception of reality and have led her into an exploration of her extrasensory abilities. Nancy spoke about her experiences to an enthralled audience at the 2017 IAND's (International Association of Near Death Studies) Conference in Denver, Colorado, and is in the process of writing a book about her profound mystical experiences.

Sacred Journeys

Regina Rivers

I grew up with five siblings. Our father was a devout Catholic and our mother, raised Southern Baptist, converted and agreed to raise us in the Catholic faith. Nothing less than a tornado or earthquake prevented us from missing Sunday mass. Prayer was an important part of my life. My childhood prayer, as far back as I can remember (which I spoke with great intention each night before I fell asleep) was "God, help me to be whatever You want me to be." I had no idea what this prayer would require of me. Whoever would have guessed that I would grow up to be a shamanic practitioner? I certainly did not. My spiritual trek from Church to now has been challenging, life transforming, exciting and quite interesting.

Before I share my personal stories with you, it's important to give you some background about the process of becoming a shamanic practitioner. While some of it may shake your sensibilities, I am here to tell you that I am alive and well. I truly enjoy living the shamanic life, as do tens of thousands of others around the world who also walk this path.

In the shamanic tradition, a person generally experiences one or more initiations. These phenomena begin with one or more life-altering experiences through which one is reborn with new eyes that can see into the mysterious realms beyond everyday living. It is believed that one does not choose to enter initiation. Rather, he—in my case *she*—is *chosen* by Spirit. Sometimes the chosen one wants to decline. If Spirit is calling and the potential initiate isn't willing, life can become intense. Spirit is much like a parent who feels the need to have the unruly child do the right thing.

This *calling* is sometimes accompanied by physical, mental, spiritual or emotional illness or dis-ease. The illness can appear for no apparent reason and cannot be healed by typical medicine. Shamanic illness can cause a person's deepest fears to surface. Confronting and moving through personal fear is a first major step. Many of us have been hard-wired into living fear-based lives as a result of frightening and traumatic childhood events.

Once her greatest fears are confronted and released, the initiate's illness most likely disappears. Healing from as many wounding experiences as possible, no matter how frightening, is important. Fear can impede us from taking responsibility for our own lives. It can also deprive us of blissful experiences. Fear is also the greatest obstacle to the initiation process.

Stepping Into Shamanic Initiation

ONE INITIATION IS PLENTY, yet a shamanic practitioner often has many throughout her life. Initiation experiences can come in dreams and visions; however, the most common form is through the process called shamanic journeying whereby the initiate is taken by spirit into other dimensions, also called non-ordinary worlds or realms. Most initiations occur in what is known as the upper world, a realm which is etheric or celestial in nature. Shamanic initiation can require years, and may be unique for each individual, yet cross-cultural hallmarks can be identified throughout. I have experienced twelve of those so far: *Upper World Experience, Unity Consciousness, Spiritual Death and Rebirth, Briefly Forgetting Personal History, Meeting a Helpful Spirit, Realizing a Sense of Purpose, Dismembering, Re-Membering, Sensing Energy, Divine Madness, Understanding Reality, and Shamanic Empowerment.*

To give you an idea of what a shamanic initiation is like,

I will share four of my own initiation journeys. The first one occurred on August 16, 1987. I experienced what I believe to be as close to a near death experience (NDE) as is possible without actually having been near death. Having read much on the subject throughout the years, I came to recognize this experience as a form of shamanic initiation. In the Eastern tradition, it would be called a Kundalini awakening, or what American psychologist, Abraham Maslow called a "peak experience." Psychiatrist, Stanislav Grof, refers to it as a "spiritual emergency." Each of these represents different traditional viewpoints for a process of awakening to spirituality.

My NDE occurred while I was deeply meditating with three other people. I simply *found* myself in another dimension. I did not *go* there, I simply was there. I was no longer Regina— mother, daughter, sister, friend—for my ego had vanished and I was completely at peace. I felt as if I were part of the whole of existence. I did not see anything other than an ocean of pure energy that completely enveloped me. It was as if I were standing inside a television set when the picture turns to snow. I did not *feel* anything until I sensed a life force very close, loving me as I have never experienced love before or since. I remember thinking *this is what death is like.*

I *heard* telepathically, *Yes, this is what it is like, but for now you must go back.*

I thought *No, no, no. I want to stay here in this wonderful, peaceful place.* And, I truly didn't know what *back* meant. This place was all I knew.

The voice expressed that I had to go back and accomplish my purpose. Although I protested, I sensed my body swooshing backwards at a rapid rate of speed, yet I was not physically moving.

I opened my eyes and was back in my body. As the other three people in the room discussed their experiences, I sat quietly, trying to understand what had just happened to me. And then, unexpectedly, every possible emotion began to pulsate through me. Tears flowed down my cheeks. I cried, then laughed hysterically. I broke into a cold sweat. My teeth chattered uncontrollably and my body swayed from side-to-side and back and forth. I wondered if I were losing my mind.

I remember my friend telling me I would be okay, to just let go and allow whatever was happening to run its course. Relaxing the best I could, I became like a rag doll, flopping every which way while the other three held me as securely as they could to prevent injury. It seems I faded in and out of reality. Afterwards, my friends told me the involuntary movements had lasted about twenty minutes.

Looking back, I now understand that what occurred was a heightened transcendental experience. This "after event" was the process of my spiritual body reincorporating with my physical form. It was as if an electric current of 220 volts was being forced through a 110-volt electrical line. My energy grid had been upgraded or re-wired! From my experience that night, I *knew* I had a purpose for being on earth. I *knew* that someday I would consciously become aware of that purpose. Until that time I would just have to be content in knowing that I was on the right path.

After that first initiation, I was guided to explore in depth and grow through many facets of spirituality. It was an exciting time for me. Then, sixteen years later, my life was again radically changed. On June 21, 2003, I met my first shamanic teacher, Tom Cowan, PhD. There are forces in both the ordinary and non-ordinary worlds that work together to bring us to the right place at the right time. As I listened to Tom speak, everything divinely clicked into place! I *knew* that in 1987 I had been reborn, given new eyes with which to see into spiritual realms, which had been guiding me along my way. On that day in 2003, I was finally ready to accept my place on the shamanic path. On that day, I realized with pure clarity that I had been perfectly led there. I felt it in my very bones. I was home!

Once an initiate accepts her place on the shamanic path, it is important to practice by helping others heal. At the same time, she cannot practice on others until, by tradition, she is given permission by a teacher. My practice and business began when

I received a call from Tom Cowan telling me that he referred me to a person who was looking for a shamanic practitioner. Since then, I have been tending to a growing clientele in my home.

A shamanic practitioner often has many initiations through-out her life. Why would this be? Usually, each is a different type of initiation, which takes the practitioner into a specific level of understanding or work. Through shamanic journeying and initiations, the practitioner is empowered with empathy and understanding of the wounds, fears and hopes of those she serves.

My second initiation occurred on March 17, 2012, during a two-year long apprenticeship program with another of my teachers, Cecile Carson, M.D. The overall personal theme of this initiation had to do with a fear-invoking childhood memory that had resurfaced within me. Confronting and moving through this obstructive fear was my necessary ultimatum. As instructed by Cecile, this immensely challenging journey required me to be spiritually dismembered or taken apart in order to be shamanically re-membered or reborn. Being re-membered, much as being reborn, refers to being spiritually put back together as who we truly are rather than who we thought or believed we were. This journey in fact did heal that childhood trauma, thus eradicating my fear surrounding it.

The third experience occurred in November 2012, deep in the Amazonian jungle of Peru. At the end of an eight-hour boat ride up the Amazon River, I was in a Shipibo village with 16 other people from around the world. We, a shaman and a medicine man, were journeying in sacred ceremony inside a rustic, circular temple. Again, I left my body. However, this time, it wasn't until I returned that I realized that I had been gone. Once I was back, I knew I had been in a "no-place" or what some call "the void." This time, though, the experience was far from blissful. I, Regina, had quite simply vanished, didn't exist! I had absolutely no memory of being alive! I was terrified!

Later, working with my Spirit Guides, I learned that I hadn't been taken anywhere outside myself. Rather I had been taken into the deepest part of myself so that I would experience what it was like to not exist and to be completely out of control. Mission accomplished! My Spirit Guides explained that my whole life up to that point had been spent holding too tightly onto control. Spirit knew this was the only way to show me how important it was for me to let go and use that energy in a much more productive way. To this day, that deep teaching reminds me that whenever I am in control mode, ego is leading the way and it is time to let go.

What Comes After Initiation or Rebirth?

GREAT RESPONSIBILITY comes with gaining access to the healing arts through shamanic initiation. Once we see the truth behind what we thought was the only reality, our world opens up to different choices. Initiations can change us in so many ways that we are finally able to let go of old behavioral patterns which no longer serve us. In short, our worlds and lives become larger because we can see beyond the ordinary world.

My Personal Benefit

MY LIFE HAS BEEN ENHANCED in countless ways since I first stepped onto the shamanic path. My greatest time of need for its sustenance came on November 21, 2017, when my beloved husband, Philip, passed suddenly and unexpectedly from a brain aneurysm. After my shock morphed into deep, deep grief, I felt temporarily paralyzed. Once I was able to start functioning somewhat again, I decided to journey. This journey, for me, became another initiation; for it delivered me into the reality of life after death.

Spiritually, I journeyed to the lower world, a *place* I go to meet with my ancestors. They were waiting in a sacred circle, as they often do. This time, as I walked toward them, I saw someone standing in the middle of the circle. It was my beloved Philip! I ran to him and we hugged and hugged and hugged. We were in awe that we were there together! He had that boyish, joy-filled smile on his face that always lit me up. He told me he was fine, and we held each other and cried. A combination of sadness, relief, deep love and utter joy flooded my heart! The love I felt from him was beyond words!

He told me he had left this world exactly the way it was meant to happen. There was nothing I could or should have done other than what I did. He didn't want me to be distressed about that any more.

At one point, I looked at him and said, "Do you realize what is happening here?"

His expression said, *What do you mean?*

I said, "You're here with me. You are really here!" Philip had not believed in an afterlife. His face held a questioning expression. I continued, "This means that you can come out of the nothingness and be with me!"

His expression slowly shifted. I knew he understood when a beautiful *aha* expression appeared! I was overjoyed to see this dawn on him!

Afterwards, Philip began visiting me in dreams. Concurrently, our granddaughter, Maddie, had been asking him to visit in her dreams. A night or so after meeting him in my journey, he fulfilled her wish. During their conversation, she asked him if he had any messages for me.

Philip said, "Tell her I saw her with the flowers and the lights."

Maddie called me the next day and was quite excited. She said, "I don't know if this means anything to you," and she delivered his message.

Little did she know that a few days earlier, I bought a dozen red roses in honor of Philip. Wanting to photograph them in a particular way, I held the bouquet in one hand and did my best to take the photo with my other hand. I had to take several shots over and over to make sure that light wasn't shining through the spaces among the flowers.

Our granddaughter's delivery of Philip's message confirmed that he was indeed with me at that time. He chose to communicate through Maddie so I would know his presence was real and not imagined. Receiving my husband's message has been a great source of comfort for me.

Perhaps this understanding was one of the most important reasons why I began to walk the shamanic path. This work has led me into realms that most people are unaware of. I have opened my mind and heart to realize that there is much more beyond this ordinary world than my five senses can fathom. I have faced and released deep fears, healed traumas and old patterns and gained knowledge that otherwise may not have occurred. Because of these journeys and initiations, my life has been transformed beyond measure.

While my concepts of religion and spirituality have greatly changed from when I first began my childhood prayer, "God help me to be whatever You want me to be," I am in awe of where I have been led. I am immensely thankful for all I have been fortunate enough to experience and now understand. I am in deep gratitude for all of my sacred journeys!

Regina Rivers is a prominent advocate for peace and spirituality in Western Pennsylvania and a Peace Ambassador for The Patrick McCollum Foundation for Peace. She resides in Allison Park, Pennsylvania, where she works as shamanic practitioner at Rivers Healing Arts, LLC. She is the founder of SITE NITE, an organization dedicated to providing a safe and sacred space where its members can experience, explore and support each other's intuitive, telepathic and spiritual gifts and also expand them. The group meets twice monthly and entertains a wide variety of speakers in an effort to raise the consciousness of humanity. Recently widowed to the late Philip Rivers, Regina is womb mother to two daughters and heart mother to a step-son and two step-daughters, all of whom earn her praise for individuality, courage and goodness. She is grandmother to seven young adults who she believes will change the world with their unique gifts and talents.

My Dream Girl

Marty Kurtyka

I've been told that I was a happy baby. Now I don't remember that far back, but I wasn't a happy child. For one, I suffered from severe allergies and asthma. During my early years, I was home alone with my grandmother, as both of my parents worked. Rather than spending time with kids my age, I became a dreamy introvert, gazing out a window.

At about age seven, I started having a recurrent dream about a girl. I wasn't interested in girls, and there was no girl in the neighborhood or at school who looked like her.

In these dreams, I saw this girl with straight, reddish-brown hair. She didn't say anything or interact with me. I just *saw* her, and oddly enough, I *smelled* her. The scent wasn't perfume. It was more a natural body smell. (It's a weird thing, but I've always been aware of the natural aromas of people's bodies.) After I awakened from the dream, her scent remained with me for a while.

Flash forward to February 1972. I was a twenty-five-year-old college graduate sharing a duplex with a roommate and working on a construction job until I figured out what I wanted to do. I had dated different girls, but I wasn't dating anyone at the time.

My roommate and I enjoyed going to clubs to hear rock bands. One bar we sometimes visited was called the Balloon Saloon. It was in a city near the Hudson River, relatively far from where I lived.

We were there on a February night. The place was packed, and the moving crowd made the room uncomfortably warm. I sat against a back wall drinking a beer and listening to the band. After a time, I headed to the bar for another drink.

Just as I got to the bar, a young, attractive woman bumped into me! She apologized profusely. I pretended to be injured as a joke. Wanting to make amends, she offered to buy me a beer. I accepted, and we started to chat. There was no room at the bar or tables, so the two of us went back to sit against the wall.

Her name was Brenda. She was about 5'7" with long, reddish-brown hair. She had a beautiful smile, and I enjoyed talking with her. We shared our personal information and later left the club to continue talking.

I felt as though I had met the girl next door, even though we didn't live in the same town. I lived in Ridgewood, and Brenda had always lived in Clifton, in a different county. *Coincidentally,* my mother had also grown up in Clifton and was also working as a nurse in a doctor's office there. *Coincidentally,* that same doctor delivered both Brenda and me and all her siblings. Also *coincidentally,* Brenda's father owned a garage next door to the doctor's office, and I *knew* her dad as well as his brother, who worked for him.

Not only did Brenda and I spend the evening together, we talked throughout the night until I drove her to her apartment around daybreak! That was the beginning of a blooming romance.

One evening, while holding Brenda close, I *recognized* her scent. It brought back those recurring childhood dreams of the girl with reddish-brown hair. I told her about them and said I was lucky to have found the girl of my dreams. Brenda then confessed that when she saw me walking toward the bar that night, she felt an immediate attraction and purposely bumped into me. (I've decided that guys are always the dumb ones who don't know what 's going on, and the girls usually have it figured out.)

Brenda and I fell in love almost immediately as a result of our "accidental" meeting. Neither of us has ever dated another person since.

The girl of my dreams and I have been happily married for forty years.

Marty Kurtyka and his wife, Brenda, reside in Wayne, New Jersey. Both are retired teachers and parents of an adult daughter. Marty has had a lifelong fascination with unexplainable happenings. This account of meeting the love of his life is one such episode.

God, If You Are Out There

Lizz Naughton

It was in the spring of 1988. I had just been accepted as a shaman's apprentice. Yorg was a world-renowned botanist and I was excited to have him as a mentor. As a part of my initiation, he asked that I go see one of his friends who had organized a gathering of women healers from all over California. I wasn't sure where I would fit in. I wasn't a healer, but I trusted Yorg, so I respected his wishes.

Saturday arrived, and I walked up to Sunflower's house. Greeting me at the door, she reminded me of Peggy Lipton from the *Mod Squad*. The living room and kitchen were filled with women laughing and trading stories about healing techniques and outcomes. I felt uncomfortable and out of place, but it was a privilege to be a part of the confidences they shared. It was foreign to me to hear about healing as an occupation. The group discussed different modalities being used throughout California. After lunch, we took a long hike, and I felt more comfortable as the day wore on. I tried to imagine what it would be like if I too were a healer, surmising I would find out once I started my apprenticeship with Yorg.

We looped around the property to a clearing that had a fire pit, large lava rocks, and a bare structure made of bent bamboo poles, making it resemble an igloo. Big, heavy blankets were hanging from the posts. We were instructed to grab the blankets and cover the structure. In the center of the hut was a big hole. I couldn't imagine what it was for, but I did what they asked. Sunflower had started a fire and was heating lava rocks. I noticed one of the ladies go into the structure with some of the blankets. She was followed by another carrying jugs of water. Finally, Sunflower started to roll the now red-hot lava rocks into the completed sweat lodge and the ladies cheered. When the last rock was rolled into place, Sunflower came out and told us where we could leave our clothes.

Oh My God! Did she mean take of my clothes? Before I had a chance to panic, Sunflower said, "Lizz, since this is your first sweat lodge, find a spot in the second row so you aren't so close to the fire. It's going to get hot in there." I smiled and nodded, secretly trying to think of an excuse to leave. The healers were taking their clothes off quickly because it was starting to get cold. I couldn't find a reason to leave, so I disrobed and got into the lodge as fast as possible. Once inside, I found the floor carpeted with soft, woven blankets. When the last healer took her seat, the flaps were lowered, leaving the outside world behind.

It was quiet for a long time before Sunflower spoke. "When we pray, it is like shooting arrows into the heavens. They will fall on people who need them most." I thought that was beautiful.

She began the prayer, and I watched as she dipped a ladle of rosemary-infused water onto the glowing rocks in the middle of the lodge floor. The first bellowing plume of mist rose from the hissing rocks. Someone behind Sunflower added to the prayer, and another ladle of water snapped and sizzled as it hit the rocks. With each ladle, the temperature in the lodge rose. I held the cloth over my nose and mouth so that I could breathe and sipped water from a jug that was given to me to stay hydrated. The lodge was hot! The first set of prayers ended and the second began; Sunflower called them *rounds*. The round that had the most significance to me was when one of the healers called out to pray for the alcoholic still suffering. That resonated through me. Alcoholism plagued both sides of my family, including my dad. It had created untold chaos and sadness in my home as I was growing up. I hoped our prayers would find and help him.

After that round the flaps of the sweat lodge were flung open, and we filed out into the darkness. It was cold and refreshing. The contrast against my skin felt nourishing, but we didn't stay outside long. Soon we filed back and began the second half of the ceremony. When we finished, we got dressed in silence and went up to Sunflower's house to eat. The room was filled with hushed voices as the women talked about the day's events; their melodic voices carried me into a deep sleep.

When I got home from the weekend, I contacted Yorg and thanked him for the amazing experience. We agreed to start my training at the beginning of June. I was going to Florida to visit my sister, so the timing was good.

I came back from Orlando a different person. I had completed ten days of "Experiential Therapy," a new modality created by Virginia Satir, which my sister Georgia was learning to use in her therapy practice. I worked with her boss, Katherine, who started the process of transforming me into a person less wounded by my history. Katherine told me that when I got back to San Diego, I would have to go to Alcoholics Anonymous in order to continue my healing. "Why do I have to go there?" I asked. "I'm not an alcoholic."

"Because they have recovery there and you need it." She was right. I didn't want to stop the momentum I had started, so I decided to check it out when I got home.

My first day back at work I found an opportunity to pull my coworker, Bob, our "recovery guy," aside and tell him I wished to attend one of his AA meetings. He laughed and said that was the best news he'd heard in a long time. I went with him that night. The meeting room was packed.

There were kids in their teens, tons of people my age, and some older members. It was not at all like I had imagined. Bob handed me a cup of coffee and began introducing me to his friends. I had no idea what they were talking about, but I felt some relief. I really liked the meeting, and I continued attending for the next two months before I realized that I was one of them. It was a little bit harder for me to identify because I wasn't an everyday drinker, nor did I lose everything because of alcohol. I was a periodic binge drinker (which means I would only drink once a month—for a week). I was allergic to alcohol, meaning that once I drank alcohol, I had a hard time stopping. That explained a lot! I was grateful to find out what was wrong with me, but I was in a constant state of upheaval. Katherine and my sister knew of my alcoholism all along but left it up to me to discover the truth. Recovery doesn't work if you are not committed to heal because it gets very real and painful.

I jumped into recovery wholeheartedly. I felt sad that I would have to let go of the apprenticeship with Yorg. I wouldn't be able to participate in the ceremonies and remain sober. I knew that recovery was going to have a deeper impact on me, for it felt incredibly spiritual and real. I wanted to have a different kind of life than what I had been living, so I decided to give it a year.

Shortly after my first anniversary, my sponsor lowered the boom and told me to find a God of my own understanding. I had been avoiding the subject for the last year with good reason. I knew there was no such thing as God. I had proof. Raised in Christian Science from childhood, I had learned that God was Love. I'd devoted myself to learning everything I could about God, but all that ended when I was twelve. My dad went missing for weeks. When he finally came home, he was jobless. Our family struggled hard to make ends meet. Where was God? I couldn't figure out why God had abandoned us and would allow my family to suffer so much and not help my Dad. The only thing that made sense to me was that there must not be a God. I put my Bible and books away that day and didn't pray again until I got in to Alcoholics Anonymous. Now I was being asked to do the impossible, but I made the effort to be respectful.

My sponsor was always talking about the power of God. I felt that it shouldn't be up to me to tell her the truth, that God didn't exist. I was in a quandary because she expected results. My greatest fear was that I would be thrown out of AA. It had been a rough year, but it was the best thing that had ever happened to me. I didn't know what to do and I didn't want to leave the very thing that was giving my life so much meaning.

Often in meetings I would hear *go ahead and pray even if you don't mean it*. I figured it couldn't hurt, so that would be a good place to start. I thought about it for a long time and came up with this simple prayer, *God, if you are out there, I demand to know, show me, without a shadow of a doubt, that you do in fact exist. I need to know that you are real. Umm, thank you.* It wasn't very humble, but it was the best I could do. I had a horrible sense of doom every time I thought about it because I already knew the truth, and I dreaded having to come to terms with that reality. That prayer had become a mantra for the next week.

Of course, nothing happened. Sunday rolled around, and I was driving home from my evening meeting. Tears started to roll down my cheeks. I had secretly hoped I was wrong, that I would have had some kind of sign that God existed. But there was none. When I got home, I turned the TV on and started to flip through channels. I landed on Barbara Walters interviewing a baseball pitcher who had been treated for cancer and was told that he would never pitch again. Against all odds, he rejoined his team. He was close to making it to the World Series when he broke his arm while pitching. The snap was so loud that the crowd could hear it throughout the stadium. The ball player's name was Dave Dravecky.

I was mesmerized by his story. Barbara changed the subject and asked the ballplayer about his faith in God and his bout with cancer. His face seemed to get softer and his eyes began to twinkle like the people I had come to know in my meetings. He began to talk about God. I started to cry, having forgotten what it was like to have a deep love for God. Apparently, it had never left me; it was just buried under my fear, disappointment, and tremendous sadness. This was the sign I had been looking for! It was as if Dave was speaking directly to me! The ballplayer was answering all the questions I had struggled with since I was a kid.

I got ready for bed with my best Scarlett O'Hara determination, *God as my witness, I'm going to San Francisco and tell*

Dave Draveky how he saved my life! A nagging thought seeped in about the fact that I had never been to San Francisco, but I wasn't going to worry about that until I got there. I had never been to Candlestick Park…but not to worry about that either. I would figure it out once I got there. I climbed into bed and fell asleep.

Monday morning met me with a new lease on life. I now had an understanding of God that I could at last build a foundation for my recovery. At work the doors for business opened and a couple made their way into the shoe department. I was alone on the sales floor, so I went over to greet them. The lady was tall, slender, and beautiful. Her husband wasn't quite as tall, and his arm was wrapped with gauze and what looked like rods and bolts protruded from it. I felt queasy looking at it. After talking to the couple, I went into the stockroom to see what I could find for her.

I had taken about ten steps inside when my coworkers surrounded me and crowded me against the workbench. They were excited, asking if I knew who I was helping. With all honesty, I didn't know who the lady was. The guys kept asking, "Do you know who's out there?" Before I could respond, one of the sales guys from next door came running down the aisle yelling "Oh my God, you guys! Do you know who's out there?" With schoolboy excitement he said, "It's Dave Draveky!"

I froze. Dave Draveky! The name reverberated through my entire body like a large, deep, gong.

I turned to face the workbench, so my coworkers couldn't see my reaction. I couldn't breathe. I held on for dear life feeling small and as expansive as the universe at the same time. At the depths of my soul, the smallest, most fragile voice said, *He heard me!* I took a breath and started upstairs to get the shoes for Mrs. Draveky. *He heard me!* This time the voice was a little bit louder. With each step I took, the voice got louder and louder: *HE HEARD ME!* Tears streamed down my face as I ascended the stairs and tried to grasp the enormity of what was happening. It was literally the eleventh hour since I had made my pledge to God that I would go and find Dave Draveky. I knew deep down that I would never go to San Francisco, let alone meet him. I had asked God to show me without a shadow of a doubt that He existed, but I never expected it to happen. I hid between the shelves and pulled myself together. The love I felt enveloping me was so intense, that it almost hurt. I was there for a long time. Finally, I grabbed some shoes and went back out to the sales floor.

I didn't share my experience with the Draveky's, but when they left I called Katherine and told her what happened. She told me not to tell anyone else because I had what AA calls a spiritual experience; the power of what happened would disappear if I told others. I took her suggestion to heart and told only my sponsor and sobriety sisters about what had happened.

Two years later, I was sitting in a meeting where two people were struggling with the concept of God just as I had. I remembered the warning Katherine had given me, and at that moment, it didn't really matter to me. If I could say something that would ease their struggle, I was willing to pay the price. At that moment I was asked to share, and I told the group how God revealed himself to me, how it happened, and how that became the foundation to building a good life. Each time I shared that story the same emotional wonderment was relived and enlarged, not diminished.

At the time of this writing, (January 2018) I am settled in New Mexico where I live with my husband. I will soon be celebrating thirty years of recovery. It hasn't always been easy; nothing worthwhile is. I now mentor others. This has also been a large part of my own healing. Several years ago, my passion for healing awakened and I got certified in Eden Energy Medicine. I am now building a practice and I like to teach. I have grown into becoming a healer, and I try to live my life today in maximum service to God and my fellows.

Looking back, I would never have imagined that this unfolding adventure would begin with my sitting butt-naked in the mountains praying for the alcoholic who still suffers, and having those arrows find their way back to me!

What I know today is that God doesn't care what we call him, so long as we do.
Namaste.

Lizz Naughton is a Clinical Practitioner in Eden Energy Medicine. Located in Albuquerque, New Mexico, she is building her practice and enjoys writing about her experiences in the realms of the spirit and healing.

Drummer

Harry Pepper

There are times and events in everyone's life that appear random or meaningless, but in the long term can be seen to have lasting effects. This story follows that beat.

It was one of the most memorable Christmas gifts I have ever received: a bright red drum set, adorned with the faces of a "cool" band I didn't know. I was five years old.

I remember playing those drums for hours at a time, *entertaining* everyone within earshot, regardless of their enthusiasm or willingness to listen. And even when there was no audience, I played anyway, to entertain myself.

A seed of inspiration had been planted in my child self that would last a lifetime. Little did I know that music and rhythm would become a foundation for my life's work, providing me with methods and opportunities to transform the lives of others. But that drum set started it all.

A couple years later, my fellow second graders and I were given the opportunity to try out different instruments to play in the school's concert band. Flutes, saxophones, clarinets, trumpets, trombones, and even a tuba were displayed before us. I quickly chose the shiny trumpet. It didn't take long to discover, though, that the asthma I'd had since birth would not provide me with the consistent breath needed to play a wind instrument. Seeing my deep disappointment, the band director offered an option to play the drums instead… if I was interested.

Interested? Of course I was interested!

He had wisely held back the drums, *knowing* that every other second grader would have selected them as their first option if given that choice. His wisdom and my asthma were additional impetus for me to pursue my early passion.

Throughout middle and junior high school, I was given opportunities to play most percussion instruments. Playing promoted deep friendships and taught me the importance of discipline, focus, self-confidence, and artistic expression. On the other hand, my classmates and I were exposed to critical, volatile, emotional, and perfectionistic music instructors, who inflicted stress and pain on students.

One particularly traumatizing afternoon stands out. My friend Kevin and I sat outside the band room as the director screamed at his students. Kevin and I learned little about music that day, but I became transfixed with questions about human behavior and how to deal with difficulties in life. My strong passion for drumming, rhythm, and music sustained me through those difficult personal encounters, but they left me with a desire to help people to heal.

As I entered college, my focus shifted to the practical pursuit of establishing career goals. I soon discovered the intriguing study of existential and humanistic psychology. I was consumed with a desire to learn about what helps people grow and why some individuals seem so stuck in their lives. My experience with multiple difficult instructors sensitized me as I chose psychology as my field of study. In the next few years, I concentrated on my own personal growth and learning to help others. However, in pursuit of my degree, I stopped playing music altogether.

During my pre-doctoral internship year, I made a new friend who happened to be writing his own music. Learning that I was a musician, Craig asked if I would accompany him on drums. In no time at all, my passion for music was reignited.

One Saturday afternoon as we were creating music together, I found myself contemplating my two areas of passion: music and healing. I wondered how I could possibly divide my time between them and simultaneously achieve the kind of expertise I desired in both areas. My dread was that I would eventually be forced to choose one over the other. I told Craig about my dilemma.

"Why don't you do both and not choose one over the other?" Craig asked.

In that simple question, I slipped into a moment where linear time seemed to stop, causing an alteration in my ordinary state of consciousness. I was fully aware that I was in my friend's apartment having a conversation, but at the same time, I was seeing both life paths, music and healing. I experienced a clear vision of the future, seeing myself playing for large audiences, music interwoven with unconditional love imbued with the power to transform lives. I realized that any separation of music and healing was rooted in my own limited thinking. I remember feeling a sense of purpose and mission and a knowing that my life was part of a larger fabric of reality.

After that awakening moment, my decisions were imbued with a newly established sense of meaning and purpose. Life seemed easier and more natural, allowing me to earn my Ph.D. (Yes, it's true. I am Dr. Pepper!) while continuing to pursue both music and healing.

I began working at the Oberlin College Counseling Center providing group and individual therapy for students. Meanwhile Craig and I continued to create and perform music. Eventually we formed a band and entertained increasingly larger audiences. My mystical experience along with my ongoing search for ways of converging my two passions led me to join a spiritual book discussion group. A book by Sandra Ingerman, *Soul Retrieval,* sparked my interest in shamanism. Reading the foreword, I learned that rhythmic patterns can induce altered states of consciousness, which engender healing. In that moment, time seemed to stop again. *Wow! This is important!* That awareness vibrated through me, and I could see a single path lighted before me.

Some friends from the spiritual group began to gather for shamanic drumming meditations known as *journeying.* I eagerly joined the group and, although that world was quite new to me, I felt safe in the nonjudgmental environment. Through those sessions, I discovered new ways of experiencing myself and life in general. I acquired a deeper connection to nature and a profound understanding and compassion for people in ways I had not previously felt, including for myself. Those meditations seemed to connect me with a higher version of me.

This new perception of reality demanded an adjustment on my part as I tried to reconcile my spiritual transformation with my ordinary daily life. At that propitious time, a friend introduced me to Shianne Eagleheart, a Native American healer, international speaker, and author of *The Wounded Bear,* a modern-day medicine story. Conversations with her along with my subsequent participation in ceremonies at her healing center validated my spiritual transformation and also enabled me to integrate my expanded consciousness with daily life.

Through continued training and experiences at the Red Bird Healing Center I learned about indigenous shamanic traditions and honed my techniques of shamanic drumming. My ongoing journeying meditations with my original group enabled me to be both the *experiencer* of shamanic drumming and the *drummer.*

For more than fifteen years now, I have been co-creating and facilitating various retreats, workshops, presentations, and lectures related to the intersection of drumming (rhythm) and healing, making use of ancient techniques, historical concepts, and the most recent research in order to assist people of all ages and populations to heal. Science research has demonstrated that a specific tempo can produce theta waves, the brainwave most associated with our dream states. Using drumming to create the rhythm that induces a "conscious dream state" allows the *dreamer* to be in a transformational state of consciousness that registers in the body, heart, and spirit, leaving one with a general sense of health and well-being.

Today, as a holistic psychologist and a shamanic drumming facilitator, I am truly blessed to be living my mission and purpose, getting to see immediate results, feeling passionate about what I do, and finally realizing that the two sacred paths of my life, music and healing, were in fact the same path the whole time.

My asthma, a health condition that had limited my life in so many ways, created the opportunity for me to learn, play, and heal though percussion and rhythm. My exposure to critical, angry band directors piqued my interest in what made people behave in aberrant ways, causing pain to others. My transformational moment in Craig's presence revealed a merging of my two passions. Reading Sandra Ingerman's book introduced me to shamanic meditation and drumming, showing me a single path. Meeting Shianne Eagleheart at the right moment provided me with the skills I needed to move forward.

I see my journey from my fifth Christmas to this day as a mystical one. I believe I was meant to be a drummer, a drummer who helps people heal.

Harry F. Pepper, Ph.D., Director of Adult Programs at Common Ground: The Cindy Nord Center for Renewal in Oberlin, Ohio, refers to himself as a psychologist and drummer. He maintains that his deepest purpose involves creating healing opportunities through music and rhythm. Harry's experience in facilitating retreats, teaching workshops, providing psychological counseling, and playing music in one of his bands has created in him a passionate and optimistic belief that every individual possesses an innate capacity to heal.

A Better Place

Frankie Sue and Cliff Newell

The original *Mystical Interludes* by Emily Rodavich inspired me to share my husband's near-death experience. I asked him if I could tell his story because I figured he would not. Here's what happened.

The date was May 17, 2000. We were building a new house and were going there do some things when Cliff got violently ill. He was sweating profusely and vomiting. I took him to the emergency room, thinking he was having a heart attack. Tests showed that a gallstone was lodged in his pancreatic duct. My husband was on the operating table early the following morning to have the stone removed. The surgeon said he would be fine in two weeks.

After surgery, Cliff was in terrible pain. Before long, a large, bluish-red spot appeared on his stomach, indicating that he was bleeding internally. On May 19th, he was life-flighted forty miles to Allegheny General Hospital in Pittsburgh. Shortly after arriving in the intensive care unit, I was called away to take a phone call from my son, who was stationed in Germany. When I returned to the ICU, Cliff was hallucinating. The doctor informed me that he had to put him in a drug-induced coma to keep him from suffering unbearable pain. He also told me to gather my family, for he didn't know if my husband would survive. He said, "All you have is prayers."

To this I replied, "If that's all I have, then he will make it."

The coma lasted for two and a half months! Day after day

and week after week, I sat by my husband's side, praying for his life. My son and his wife had been home for a while, but had to return to Germany. All we had going for us was prayers.

Each day the medical staff told me there was no change in his progress. Our thirty-forth wedding anniversary came and went with me by his side. The priest from our church came and gave Cliff last rites. My sister had a prayer chain going. I was told that all of Canonsburg prayed for him. I learned later that one of the seniors at Canon McMillan high school, where he photographed students, gave a talk about Cliff. He told what a wonderful person Cliff was and how he always encouraged teens to follow their dreams to bigger and better things after graduation. (I had to hire seven photographers to do the work that Cliff did by himself!)

After two and a half months, I finally asked the doctor to take him out of the coma. He warned that Cliff might be in a lot of pain or he could be blind, or he could be brain dead. I insisted, thinking my husband would not want to go on, especially if he were brain dead. They said it would take a week.

The month was August when Cliff came out of the coma. The first thing I said to him was, "You know I love you very much." He shook his head yes. Miraculously, he was back! At first he couldn't see, but his sight soon returned.

In September, after a few other health challenges and rehab, Cliff came home to our new house. We celebrated his sixtieth birthday on October 8th, giving thanks that he had survived his ordeal with no serious health problems. To this day I still say it was prayer that pulled him through. We all promised that if he lived, we would not yell at him again. (At least, we tried.)

He never spoke about his near-death experience until one day he said to me that he knew there was a better place. After he was out of danger, I remembered his doctor telling me that Cliff had "been around the bend" several times during his coma, meaning that his heart had stopped beating.

About three months after he was back working at the photography studio, a grieving customer told Cliff that her husband had passed away about a month before, and she didn't think she could go on. Cliff spoke up and told her about his near-death experience. He reassured her that there was a better place. Later she let us know how grateful she was that he shared his experience. It made her feel much better. (I was shocked that he told it because Cliff never talked about his experience.)

* * *

Editor's Note: After Frankie Sue shared her husband's story, she managed to convince him to talk with me on the phone. Here is Cliff's own account.

* * *

WHEN I WAS BEING LIFE-FLIGHTED in the helicopter, I had a feeling that I was going to die. This might sound strange, but in that short time, I seemed to remember everything I said to others in my lifetime.

Later, I was standing on a town square that reminded me of Munich, Germany. The stones under my feet were whitish like Belgian brick or Omani stone. I was in perfect health, feeling more alive than ever! Before me loomed a sphere of beautiful light surrounded by a kind of foggy haze. I felt overwhelming peace. I also felt love coming from within me. I was drawn to the light.

As I started to walk forward, somebody on my left put his hand on my shoulder. I could only see the side of his face, but it appeared to be a man.

He said, "You have to go back."

That's all I can remember.

Months after I was out of the hospital I went back to visit my caretakers. One of the nurses asked me if I had an out-of-body experience while I was in the coma. I told her I had. She confessed to me that my heart had stopped several times, and they "shocked" me back.

What is significant about what happened is the way it changed me. For one thing, I had never liked the sight of a hearse or funeral. If I saw a hearse parked in front of the church,

I'd cross the street. After my experience, I completely lost my fear of death. Now, I know that funeral homes, caskets, and hearses are not a part of death at all!

I also lost value of material things. I realize that relationships are the most important things in life. I also appreciate things I used to take for granted.

Here are two things that stuck with me. When we were coming home from rehab, Frankie Sue noticed debris along the road and referred to it as garbage. Oddly, the scene before me looked like art work! One evening my family and I returned home after being out for the evening. It was raining. Everybody got out of the car and went into the house. I stayed in the car and sat for a while because I loved hearing the rain. That would not have happened before I had my experience.

Yeah, my experience changed me in different ways. The best of those is that I now know there's a better place ahead.

Frankie Sue Mirisciotti Newell and her husband Cliff are the proprietors of Mirisciotti Photography in Canonsburg, Pennsylvania. The Newells, well known and well loved in their community, are the parents of Michelle and Chris. Michelle runs the photography studio along with Cynthia, granddaughter of the Newells. Chris, a retired Army veteran lives with his wife LeAne and their two daughters, Melissa and Jessica, in Springfield, Virginia.

Aunt Kay's Last Words

Anonymous

Growing up I was always close to my Aunt Mary Kay. She was my father's sister, a creative, talented music teacher. I lived with her and her husband during my first year of college and my first year of teaching. Following her retirement she gave piano and voice lessons and directed the church choir. After her husband passed she decided to give up the responsibility of caring for her large historic home, which had been part of the Underground Railroad, and move into an apartment in Washington, Pennsylvania.

Years later, as Aunt Kay's health was in decline, my husband and I bought a house nearby where she could live under the watchful care of family. She was able to move throughout the house with a walker and sit on the sunny deck to watch the antics of her back-yard birds. Friends from high school and church would stop by to remember good times or catch up. We celebrated her eightieth birthday there.

Eventually my dear aunt was diagnosed with cancer and was moved into a nursing facility for care. As she approached the end of her life, she chose to return home. Family members took turns staying with her and tending to her needs. Her worsening condition diminished her mind and memory. Often Aunt Kay was unable to recognize the loved one attending her.

One morning in December when I arrived to replace my daughter Lynn, who had spent the night, a remarkable thing happened. Lynn, a nurse by profession, was dressed in her scrubs and sweatshirt, ready to leave for the hospital. She and I were standing at Aunt Kay's bedside. I was speaking to my aunt, but my words were ignored. She glanced up at my daughter and patted her stomach.

"You're going to have a baby!" she uttered.

We assured her that the "puffery" stomach was just Lynn's bulky sweatshirt. Lynn and I passed the remark off as a side effect of the pain meds.

After attending candlelight service on Christmas Eve, I joined my cousin who had stayed with Aunt Kay. A former choir member and his daughter visited and lovingly sang "O Holy Night," which my aunt had taught. My sister, a nurse, arrived to spend the night with us. Aunt Kay fell asleep. She passed quietly on Christmas day.

After our days began to return to normal routines, my daughter Lynn came to talk. She wanted to share with us that on the day after Christmas she took a pregnancy test. The result was positive! Thinking she had bungled the test, she repeated it. The result was the same each time.

Somehow, Aunt Kay knew.

Editor's Note: This author preferred not to use her name. I verify the authenticity of this story.

GOD-WON

Ed Borowsky

*W*hen does coincidence, after a series of coincidences, reveal itself not to be coincidence after all?

On a Sunday, at approximately 9:20 a.m. on a sunny, cloudless October morning in Winter Springs, Florida, I pulled out of a parking lot. I turned left onto a residential road, and as I rolled to a stop at the red light, a car whizzed by on State Road 434. I can still see the image years later as a short video clip in my mind: a car driving by in front of me, from left to right, the car moving fast. It caught my attention.

"Odd," I thought.

I turned right on red, and as I drove on State Road 434, I approached from behind the only car on the road—the car that had passed. As I got closer and the license plate came into focus, I did a double take. On the left side of the white Florida plate, it read GOD. But I couldn't make out the right side of the vanity tag until I sped up and pulled closer to the rear end of the vehicle. The license plate read, GOD-WON.

The words had a profound impact on me. *Was this a coincidence?* I had just left the synagogue after I had stood-up for the first time to recite the Mourner's Kaddish for my father who had passed away ten days earlier. He died at ninety-one during Rosh Hashanah, the Jewish New Year.

For those who are not versed in the Jewish holidays, we follow the lunar calendar, not the solar calendar. It was 2014, or the Jewish year 5775. It's Jewish tradition that God opens the Book of Life for the upcoming year on the first day of Rosh Hashanah. On the tenth day God closes the book, sealing our fates for the upcoming year. That is the last day, the holiest of days known as Yom Kippur, also known as the Day of Atonement. Jews look back at their actions of the past year and look forward to the year to come. It's a holiday of reflection, and one of projection, and in so doing the Jew hopes that God will write him or her, their family and friends into the Book of Life for a happy, healthy, and prosperous New Year.

My father died and was laid to rest the day before Yom Kippur in the Abraham Lincoln National Cemetery in Elwood, Illinois. Because of obligations, I had to fly home to Orlando the day after Yom Kippur. I had no choice. I flew home that Saturday evening.

I had a compelling desire to say Kaddish for my father. I awoke early to attend the morning-prayer session or minyan, which is held every Sunday morning at our synagogue at 9 a.m.

The Mourner's Kaddish is recited when there is a minyan (a quorum of ten people over the age of thirteen). It's believed that saying Kaddish is of great merit for the soul who has passed away. Many believe that our actions in the physical world affect those who have passed on to the spiritual world.

The prayer makes no mention of death, loss or mourning; nor is there any reference to the person who died. Kaddish speaks only of the greatness of God. Many believe the soul ascends and is judged according to its deeds on earth. Everything accomplished by the soul, both positive and negative, is carefully considered. When in the midst of judgment, the words of Kaddish ascend, uttered by those who grieve.

Reciting Kaddish honors the departed and keeps their memory alive. Saying the hallowed words of Kaddish is the ultimate sign of love and respect one can offer for those who have passed away.

There weren't enough people to make a minyan, so I didn't get the opportunity to recite the Mourner's Kaddish that Sunday morning.

The next day, determined to honor my father, I awoke early

to attend the weekday minyan held at the Jewish Community Center beginning at 7:45 a.m. That Monday, Tuesday, and Wednesday, once again, we didn't have enough people to make minyan. Each day I left disappointed and I was beginning to feel that I was failing him. On Wednesday evening another Jewish holiday began. This meant that my saying the Mourner's Kaddish had to be postponed for another four days. I was frustrated but still determined.

Finally, that following Sunday morning, there were enough people for me to stand up and recite Kaddish. It was difficult for me to get through the prayer, but once completed, I had a profound sense of pride that I had fulfilled my obligation. Dad would have been proud.

I drove off in my car. That's when I followed the car with the GOD-WON plate until it passed through the red light. I didn't make the light and had to stop. While waiting for the light to change, I glanced down at my cell phone to check my email. My eyes focused on what was to be the second coincidence. The only unread message, from Psalm51@yahoo.com, stood out at the top of my screen like a beacon!

The light changed, and I continued on my drive home, but suddenly I had an overwhelming, strange feeling. I clicked on the email link, and all I could find was a link to a penny stock solicitation. I *had* to pull over and Google Psalm 51.

After reading the psalm, tears came. I sat there trying to comprehend what it meant. The essence of the psalm was, I had sinned in my life. My path forward was to understand my transgressions, cast them aside, and move forward for the rest of my life with a pure heart. I would serve God, and in so doing I would find my redemption.

I arrived home. My wife was sitting at our kitchen table, which overlooked our backyard. I began telling her what happened. As I was explaining the series of events that had unfolded on my way home, she spoke in an excited whisper, "Look, Look…!"

Outside the kitchen window in a hanging flower basket perched a large red cardinal. The brown female was nearby. We were motionless for a moment until my wife rose, walked to the sliding glass door with her cell phone, and snapped a picture of the resplendent bird. Soon after the click, the birds flew off. I was overwhelmed with a feeling I can't adequately describe.

A few minutes later my cell phone rang. It was my sister who lives in Lancaster, Pennsylvania. She was calling to tell me that she was looking out her window at beautiful cardinals in her backyard. She said she felt my father's presence and was compelled to call me.

Was the first thing I came across after saying Kaddish for my father—a car with a vanity plate that said GOD-WON a coincidence?

Was the email that read Psalm51@yahoo.com in bold print at the top of the screen, a coincidence?

Was that beautiful cardinal in the flower basket outside my window, a coincidence?

And then the call from my sister, was that a coincidence too?

It has been three years since his passing, and I've just signed a contract with a publisher to have my first book published. Was it a coincidence that I told my story to her and she asked if I would be interested in writing about this series of coincidences for this inspirational book about stories like mine? Is it a coincidence that you have read this? Perhaps, but I believe, perhaps not!

We get caught up in the fast pace of our lives, and we fail to slow down and listen. Perhaps we need to take a deep breath and allow God to come to the forefront of our lives. Perhaps we move too fast, or we're not listening hard enough to realize that divinity is all around and will reveal itself when we're in the frame of mind to receive it.

If you were moved reading this, I promise this chain of events did occur to me that Sunday morning. They have changed my life profoundly. I am happier than I've ever been and can say now like I couldn't say before, I acknowledge that in my limited comprehension there is one God, the beauty indescribable, and I know my parents are within God's embrace. It was revealed to me that morning that everything in my life was just fine.

And there is one last thing I'd like to share. I came across this poem during that time. A coincidence?

Our yesterdays are beyond the reach of death,
When our love transforms them into living influences.
Thus we continue to be guided by a light
Which transcends time and defies death.[1]

Ed Borowsky is the author of *The Great Mongolian Bowling League of the United States of America* and other novels. Retired from a long business career, he lives in Winter Park, Florida, with his wife, Michele. They are parents to three adult sons. In his former life, Ed wrote copy for his full-service advertising agency in Boston. Now he devotes his time to writing novels, the fabric of which are interwoven with threads of complex human relationships. His stories are interspersed with both wit and wisdom. Visit www.EdBorowsky.com.

---

1 "Beyond Time" by Morris Adler is found on page 669 in the prayer book *Siddur Hadash,* published by The Prayer Book Press, Media Judaica of New York and Bridgeport, Conn.

Finding Joy with My Fairy Ally

Maura McCarley Torkildson

Loving ourselves creates room for joy. Self-acceptance means *I unashamedly love what I consider to be the best parts of me too.* When I think of joy, I realize that it is the small things that sustain me, the little joys. We are culturally set up to look for big, dramatic successes and we often miss how important the small joys are.

Recently I took a class, *Awakening to Our Fairy Kin,* offered by my friend and priestess Marguerite Rigolioso. During the class she led us through a visualization to meet our fairy ally. In this visualization, after traveling through the veil to the magical forest of the Fae, I met my fairy ally. My ally appeared in my inner vision like a Brian Froud pixie (if you want a visual, look up Ffaff the Footer). He/she (the gender is very fluid) revels in silliness. Marguerite instructed us to ask for the ally's name.

I heard, *"My name is Ally Sheedy."*

Somewhat abashed, I responded, *"What? That is the name of an 1980s actress."* On further reflection I realized the ingenuity of the name. The name Ally, a direct reference to ally/supporter. Sheedy references the Irish name for fairy folk, *The Sidhe* (pronounced shee). Ally (alley) is also a passage way, or portal from one place to another, as in *he is my portal to fairy land.* The multiple meanings of this name confirmed for me Ally Sheedy's validity. I giggled with glee, thrilled to have my new inner friend.

Ally Sheedy has been with me ever since. His entrance into my life is much like the return of a lost childhood companion. Ally's silliness is my joy. He likes to sit on the hot tub cover when I am soaking. He sits on the edge of the hot tub cover, torso-less, showing only his swinging crossed legs adorned with his favorite Pippi Longstocking-type leggings and pointed fairy shoes. Other times he dances a jig for me. Occasionally she shows up in pink fairy dresses (gender shifts intentional here). I am compelled to honor him every day at my fairy altar under our oak tree in the backyard.

I share with my family what Ally Sheedy pops in to say now and then. My daughter Megan thinks I am nuts (secretly, I think she relishes my strangeness). My mischievous side adores the expressions I get in response. This puckish silliness is an inheritance from my father's side of the family. Growing up, Megan was often subjected to my inane whims when I drove her to high school in the morning. I regaled her with different voices, accents, and crazy characters, much like my father used to do when he was driving. Like he did, I relished the responses—rolled eyes, shaking head, "my crazy mom" cringes.

I once asked my partner, Pete, why he never teases me about my relationship with Ally Sheedy, the latest addition to my repertoire of eccentricity. He sighed and responded, "I like having you around, so I just accept it. The alternative is sending you off to an asylum and that is not acceptable."

Ally Sheedy is real to me. I know this is unconventional in this world, but I love my relationship with Ally Sheedy and all the unfettered joy it brings me. My self-love allows me to accept and express my peculiarities even if they make me vulnerable to the criticism of naysayers or people who think I should act like an "adult." Joy is the natural result of childlike wonder to the small things we often miss when adulting. In fact, I need this joy to sustain me in the face of the state of this world. Like all other emotions, joy (and its offshoot silliness) is our birthright as humans. I refuse to deny myself my unique forms of joy for the sake of convention.

Our emotions—every single one of them—are part and parcel of the experience of being human. It comes with the package. Our souls understand the importance of emotions to our growth, even when our minds do not.

Maura McCarley Torkildson, author of *The Inner Tree: Discovering the Roots of Your Intuition and Overcoming Barriers to Mastering It,* is also a speaker, an artist, an intuitive, and a Soul Creativity Support Mentor. Her work includes supporting creatives and spiritual women entrepreneurs to complete their creative soul projects. She is a Certified Professional Co-Active Coach and has an M.A. in Women's Spirituality from New College of California. Her artwork has been exhibited in both the U.S. and Malta. Come visit Maura at MauraTorkildsonCoaching.com.

Messages from Drake

Patty Fujimoto

Traditionally we provide a big dinner on Christmas Eve and also on Christmas day at our family-owned restaurant, the Hana Hou. For the first time I was solely responsible for seeing things through. My husband and partner, Drake, had passed earlier in the year. Knowing that I had a super hard day ahead, I woke up stressed on the morning of Christmas Eve. Before starting my day, I silently asked Drake to please be with me to get me through the holiday.

Reporting in at the restaurant, I was greatly relieved to find that everything was going pretty darned good. Taking that as an opportunity, I rushed back home to feed the dogs and let them run for a while.

Our house is in a private wooded area where nobody lives nearby or visits without invitation. The yard is fenced in, and a gate stands at the entrance to our home. As I exited through the gate for the second time that day, I happened to look down. An unusual black plastic-looking rectangle, about three-fourths inch by two inches lay on the ground. I picked it up and turned it over. Engraved in gold script stood a single word: *nautilus*. Upon seeing that familiar word I *knew* Drake was with me!

A few days before my husband died he was in a phase where he was seeing things, meeting people, and having what he called spiritual dreams. He woke up out of a dead sleep one night and told me about an especially vivid dream.

In the dream he was swimming in a blue ocean of crystal

clear water. Up from the depths came a nautilus. Drake reached out and touched it. He was awed by the dream. I felt that it was symbolic and meaningful. Not only had it stayed with me, I had been thinking about that dream on and off for three days prior to finding the small rectangle.

I had walked through that gate two times earlier that day, and now there it was—a definite *I'm here* conveyed by the word *nautilus*. There was no other explanation.

To top it off, I got through that day, the next, and Christmas week just fine with little or no stress. It felt like Drake was there making sure nothing went off the rails.

That wasn't the first time Drake reached out from the other side of the veil. There were at least two other occasions when he made his presence known.

Not long after my husband passed, a black duck suddenly appeared in my friend's yard and lingered. She called and said, "A black duck came and flew around the yard for three days. I knew it was Drake letting us know he's here. (A male duck is called a Drake.)

Another event occurred at Drake's ash scattering. We were twenty-four in number gathered at a pebble beach where there are different types of rocks in various sizes and shapes. Drake's daughter cried uncontrollably.

"What's going on?" I asked. "Why are you crying so much? Are you upset about something?"

She said, "I just didn't talk to my dad enough!"

I knew she was experiencing terrible remorse. She and her dad had been estranged.

I said, "Well, you can always talk to him…you'll just have to listen for the answer in a different way."

"What do you mean by that?" she asked.

Thinking of what to say, I looked down at the ground. My eyes focused on a heart-shaped lava rock. No mistaking, a heart-shaped lava rock! There it lay, right at my feet!

Pointing at the ground, I said, "Like that, Dear!" I picked up the rock, warm from the sun, and handed it to her. "Here's a heart—a message from your dad to us."

She took the small, warm, heart and held it close. Her face relaxed, and she obviously felt better.

She later passed the heart rock back to me. I still have it along with many precious memories of Drake.

Patty Fujimoto and her husband, Drake, were doubly blessed by their compatible, successful relationships in both marriage and business. They were the proprietors of the Hana Hou in Na' Alehu, Hawaii, the southernmost restaurant in the United States, until Drake died in 2015. Patty, a strong and generous member of her community, continues to run the business successfully.

Rescue

Sara Holden

This morning at 0700, as in any morning whereas I do not have obligations, I meet up with my old, leaky, aluminum rowboat on Lake Lucas. It's just me, the boat and two wooden oars on a lake as still and silent as I need it to be for this ritualistic escape I engage in for peace and wellness. At this time of morning, the sun has already risen and there is a slight fog that just touches the surface of the water and rises up, enveloping the tiny, mountainous forest surrounding the lake.

Due to the leaks in the boat, I usually spend about fifteen minutes bailing out the ten inches of water with the cut-off laundry detergent bottle I stole from the abandoned boat in the next slip. As I stand in the stagnant water, bailing it out, I remind myself that this is not a big deal and I'll be so glad when we get rowing.

So it begins…. I row, and row, oftentimes having to add in a right stroke every three strokes to stay on course, for my left must be stronger. I realize I am unaligned and out of balance, but I have peace at this time. I tell myself, "knowing is half the battle." Nobody is telling me I am doing it wrong today or if I did it this way it would be so much "better." "What is better anyway?" I ask myself.

Out of the corner of my eye, I see a flicker in the lake. As I focus on the broad-winged, brilliantly orange-hued object about twenty feet across the water, I realize it is a Polyphemus Moth struggling, drowning and with all its might trying to get out of the water. I row over to her and as I stretch over the bow of the boat and extend the oar, she barely attaches herself for a minute before taking off in glorious flight for a good thirty feet, until again, the water meets her legs and she hits again, struggling, drowning. I watch for a minute contemplating whether or not to help her. I feel empathy for this moth at this moment and of course decide if I do nothing else worthwhile on this lake this morning, I will help this creature rather than be a spectator of its death.

So again, I row over to it but this time I get my fishing net and gently scoop it up and rest it on the bench in front of me. It's like a child, it's like an adult, struggling to survive, ambitious to make an impact, making it harder than it has to be. She has a tear in her wing and can't get to the land without a helping hand. She was not alone out there and neither was I. Moth and I row back to our slip where I dock my leaky old boat and walk her to the shade of a grand old black walnut tree. I rest her weary little body under the tree and she stops shaking and rests on the soft bed of soil. The moth feels better and so do I.

There is the usual couple on the pier because it is approaching 0900. They tell me that moths always die after they lay their eggs. I smile and walk towards my boat saying to myself, "Maybe this one has not laid its eggs yet."

I took that statement and applied it to myself, realizing, if purpose were eggs, I haven't laid my eggs yet either. I was struggling with a major life decision to leave teaching or not. While I knew I could survive in the current position as a seventh grade ELA teacher, essentially, that is all I would be doing, outside of splashing around like this moth, exhausted, flapping my wings struggling to keep my head above data-driven instruction. Truly, this could not be my purpose!

I would certainly not be flying or positively influencing the lives of amazing, unlimited, potential-filled young adults. My hands were tied. Instead of being able to use classic literature or novels, which I knew would engage my students, I was being required to function as their testing facilitator. Any efforts to make constructive changes were rejected by leadership. I felt that by staying, I was being complacent (a dirty word in our house) and becoming a part of the problem with public education.

Whereas beforehand I would say I was the oar and the students were the moth, as I reflect now, I was in fact the moth. The oar was my freedom to decide to leave a toxic teaching situation. I know that the gifts and talents of students cannot simply be measured on a common assessment. I needed to save myself from the data-driven leadership along with administration wanting to further their personal careers at the cost of student fulfillment. That environment was like waves and water holding me down, soaking and tearing my wings and drowning me.

Two weeks after my rowing experience, I was visited by two owls after praying for wisdom. I had lost my mom on my thirty-ninth birthday, which was five months prior to all of this happening,. The owls were the affirmation that I needed to follow my heart and use my innate wisdom as well as the encouragement that my mom would've spoken to me, had she been alive to respond to me verbally. Also, within that two-week timeframe, my principal pulled me aside again and took the final clip to my wings when she told me to not spend anymore instructional time on writing with my students because writing was not tested. The moth, the owls, and the principal's last clipping of taking writing out of my curriculum all combined to give me the confidence to resign. I submitted my letter of resignation the next week.

It has been over a year since those mystical encounters with my friend, the moth, that beautiful morning and the visit from two owls in the dead of night during my restlessness. December 9th, 2016, was my last day of teaching in a public school classroom.

What has unfolded over the last year I could never have even dreamed up. I've become the proud hostess of a successful Airbnb my husband completed the week I resigned. I am host to traveling poets, teachers, world famous filmmakers, photographers, doctors, scientists, athletes, book publishers, children, adults, and pets, and I've met more students of life than I could ever imagine along with lifelong teachers and mentors. All this from an off-grid cabin in our woods that I decorate with the words of Whitman, Emerson, and Thoreau. I serve a pot of coffee with cream and sugar each morning and clean up after each splendid visitor. I teach computer literacy and digital engagement classes part time for a private company whose mission caters to the elderly and disabled populations. I have authored my first book, *Child, You Are More Than a Number*, about all children being valued for their unmeasurable gifts,

I haven't seen an owl since those nights, nor had I seen one prior to those two visits. And even as much as I still row, I've never met up with another moth. Thankfully, I haven't had any encounters with my former principal either!

Lastly and most gratefully, my disabled wing has healed, allowing my heartfelt purpose and soul to fly, unbounded.

Sara Holden is a combat veteran, teacher and author of *Child, You Are More Than a Number*. She delights in her days alongside her husband of twenty-two years and three, almost-grown children in the twenty-three acres of woods at their homestead in North Carolina. Sara's mystical encounter with the Polyphemus Moth that day while rowing her boat on a nearby lake was the catalyst to launching her writing career and hospitality business. Her off-grid cabin, Peach's Paradise, was hand-built by her husband, Greg, from their own timber and has been host to numerous adventurers, including our publisher, Penelope Love. Sara loves this type of collaboration and is grateful for this newfound connection embracing her family and writing.

ACKNOWLEDGMENTS

When I think of the caring persons who came forth to share their mystical interludes, my heart fills with gratitude. They have woven precious fragments of their lives into this book. Their stories reaffirm our spiritual connections with the Divine and with each other. Their mystical interludes have opened new windows into their souls and also expanded their perceptions of reality. Without their committed efforts, this book would not be possible.

My tasks of collecting and editing stories have been tirelessly aided by the love and support of my two best friends, Jim Flenniken and Nancy Aloi.

Jim, my soul partner and beloved companion, inspired me to write my memoir *Mystical Interludes, An Ordinary Person's Extraordinary Experiences,* which led to inviting others to share their stories for this book. I am thankful for his good-natured presence and his willingness to read my ramblings and offer advice when asked. I can't neglect the fact that Jim takes up many of my household chores when I'm in a crunch. All these, along with his zany wit and spontaneous sense of humor, have carried me to the finish line.

Nancy, my soul sister, is always there when a need arises. When I imagine what an angel might be like, I think of Nancy. She is caring and mindful in her service to others. When my first book was published, Nancy arranged and hosted a better-than-I-could-have-hoped-for author event in my community. From that time until present, she has assisted me at book talks. If that weren't enough, Nancy has submitted her own story for this book and devoted many hours to proofreading the manuscript.

Behind the scenes, offering constant guidance and support, is my editor/publisher, Penelope Love of Citrine Publishing. Penelope's telephone voice always exudes caring and good cheer. It doesn't matter how stacked her plate might be, she never fails to answer an email or return a call. This highly competent and trusted professional woman, Penelope, delivers services that no amount of money could ever compensate.

Finally, I am ever grateful to Suzanne Giesemann for writing the eloquent Foreword to this book. She gave precious time and attention to reading my first book and also the manuscript for this one. Her energy is seemingly inexhaustible. Author of at least ten books, Suzanne educates countless people through her workshops, classes, webinars and conference appearances. First and foremost, she is a highly respected evidential medium, proving beyond a doubt that our departed loved ones are still with us in spirit. Living her life in perpetual service to grieving survivors, especially parents, Suzanne is a shining light in our world.

Thank you, all.

CALL FOR SUBMISSIONS

HAVE YOU EVER HAD A MYSTICAL INTERLUDE?

Readers of Emily Rodavich's first book, *Mystical Interludes: An Ordinary Person's Extraordinary Experiences,* responded with the stories that generated this second edition. This fuels the author's belief that everybody experiences mystical interludes to some degree. In her direct experience, strong evidence indicates that the more we share them through discussion and writing, the more they show up in our lives.

Ms. Rodavich's goal is to inspire everyone to take heed of these important events when they happen. They are important because they remind us that we are more than our bodies and minds. We are immortal spirits, each of us a particular expression of the Divine. Such experiences increase our awareness of Spirit working in and through our lives, reminding us that we are one with each other.

Mystical interludes transcend religious divisions, for they occur universally to people of faith and no faith alike, yet they validate core principles of love, forgiveness, and eternal life.

If you have had many mystical interludes, Ms. Rodavich encourages you to write a book about them. If you have experienced fewer than that, please consider submitting a description of your experience for potential publication in *Mystical Interludes III.* Visit www.mysticalinterludes.com for information.

Finally, if you are inclined to leave a review where you purchased *Mystical Interludes* or *Mystical Interludes II,* and/or on any other social media websites where you participate, your valuable feedback will help shape our next edition.

www.MysticalInterludes.com

PUBLISHER'S NOTE

Thank you for reading *Mystical Interludes II*. Please pass the torch of connection by helping other readers find this book. Here are some suggestions for your consideration:

- Write an online customer review wherever books are sold

- Gift this book to family and friends

- Share a photo of yourself with the book on social media and tag #MysticalInterludes

- Bring in Emily Rodavich and/or any of the story authors as a speaker for your club or organization

- Suggest *Mystical Interludes II* to your local book club, and download the *Book Club Discussion Questions* from www.CitrinePublishing.com/bookclubs

- Submit a story and connect with the editor by visiting www.MysticalInterludes.com

www.ingramcontent.com/pod-product-compliance
Lightning Source LLC
Chambersburg PA
CBHW021619270326
41931CB00008B/768